ENDORSEMENTS

God has embedded into this book a supernatural grace to understand His heart for children! Have you ever been moved by the cry of a newborn? The bubbling joy of a toddler? The endless energy of an adolescent? The quizzing curiosity of a child? Then you will be stirred deeply by *A Child Will Lead Them*. Jocelyn Pence has given us a tremendous insight into the beauty of children and how our Heavenly Father esteems them. After reading this book, you will come away a different person. Expect something to stir within you as you turn the pages of this unique and highly engaging book. *A Child Will Lead* US back to the heart of God! Enjoy!

–Brian Simmons
The Passion Translation Project

I first began reading these pages expecting Jocelyn to teach me about children, how they think, and how we adults can impart our wisdom to them.

How surprised and delighted I was when Jocelyn did not attempt to teach me anything. Instead, she carried me into her world where she experiences the hearts of children. With her words, Jocelyn took my heart in her hand and carried me into tiny, innocent hearts—a place I have never been before. She took me where she lives and loves. She let me see wonder in precious eyes, and then, through those eyes. I found myself not knowing if I was looking through children's eyes or through Jocelyn's eyes.

From there I peered at wonders too intimate, too pure for me. I wanted to blush. Now I understand better what Jesus meant when He said, "These children have angels constantly beholding the face of the Father."

–Harold R. Eberle
Author and President, Worldcast Ministries

In *A Child Will Lead Them*, Jocelyn Pence reminds us that we live in a complicated world where children unfortunately have been minimized and marginalized in many ways. Jocelyn has beautifully distilled the wisdom she has received from her up-close and personal interaction with children, showing us that they are not just to be taught, but often really are our teachers.

You will never see children the same after reading this book. Thank you, Jocelyn, for sharing your heart so intimately. As a leader, I was inspired in new ways to learn from the little ones.

–Dr. Randall Worley
Author of *Brush Strokes of Grace* and *Wandering and Wondering*

At 73, I don't think too much anymore about kids, even though I have 3 kids, 9 grandkids, and 3 great grandkids. The days of training have passed me by. However, I know what it is like to go through challenging times with your kids. My wife and I went through a time of darkness as our kids were trying to find their way. Thankfully, they rose out of the darkness of those days and are living an amazing life.

We were helped immensely by books written by Dr. James Dobson back in the 70s and 80s. This is a new day and we need new voices that speak to this generation. I am so thankful for Jocelyn's passion and compassion for this generation of parents and kids. Jocelyn has tapped into some great secrets that will help this generation. She is so right when she writes the words, "The secrets of the Kingdom are hidden in children. They are able to teach us with wisdom."

Too often, children are pushed aside and ignored by the church. If Jocelyn has her way, it will no longer happen.

This book is written with the pen of a passionate person who loves this generation and has been given the wisdom to instruct parents and encourage the next generation. I am thankful for the tool that Jocelyn has provided. Now, we must do everything we can to get it into the proper hands.

–Don Milam
Acquisitions Consultant, Whitaker House Publishers
Author, *The Ancient Language of Eden*

A Child Will Lead Them by Jocelyn Pence confirms why children are the teachers God gives to parents. When did we stop listening to their hearts? Could childlike faith be what Jesus is looking for in His saints when He returns to Earth? The faith of a child who only believes and doesn't know how to doubt. Open this book and discover why the word "adult" is not in the Bible.

–Bill Yount
Author and speaker

My first recollection of Jocelyn was in 2008 at an Outreach at Chambersburg High School. It was the smile attached to her heart that I will never forget. She is called to children. It is not a stepping stone, but a call, filled with heart and anointing. When you talk of children, she lights up; she knows them and treats them as they are mature adults. They are spirits who are alive, whose bodies have not matured yet, and she lives to let them be children, but especially, children of God in residence. I endorse her heart and her anointing. The Kingdom needs this book.

–**Dr. R. Brian Kisner D.D.**
Director, Legacy School of Supernatural Ministry, Tampa Florida
Author, *The Watchman on the Wall: Intercession*

A CHILD WILL LEAD THEM

A CHILD WILL LEAD THEM

EMBRACING THE FATHER'S HEART
FOR CHILDREN

Jocelyn Pence

eGenCo

eGenCo

eGenCo
824 Tallow Hill Road
Chambersburg, PA 17202, USA
Email: info@egen.co
Website: www.egen.co

 facebook.com/egenbooks   youtube.com/egenpub
 egen.co/blog   pinterest.com/eGenDMP
 twitter.com/egen_co   instagram.com/egen.co

Cover photography by Jennifer Nikole Wright (justwrightphotography.com)

Library of Congress Cataloging-in-Publication Data

Library of Congress Control Number: 2019916905

ISBN: 978-1-68019-004-5 Paperback
      978-1-68019-005-2 eBook
      978-1-68019-006-9 eBook

Printed in the United States of America

DEDICATION

This book is dedicated to the spirit of children all over the world. I believe in you. May you be free. May you be seen rightly, as our Father created you and will forever see you.

Change us. Change our world. We receive you and want to walk with you into every promise of the Lord.

TABLE OF CONTENTS

FOREWORD

I feel sorely ill-equipped to write a foreword for this book. Conviction has a way of disarming us to the point where we simply don't know what to do. And the more of this book I read, the more convicted I became.

Too often my attention whisks by children, landing upon the adults, the "important" ones. How foolish. How utterly void of heavenly perspective. It's not that there is anything wrong with the adults. It's the debilitating, subconscious thought pattern that real conversation stops when you have to bend down to have it.

And here's the truth: many of the most real, raw, and honest conversations I have had took place when I stopped, stooped, and engaged a child. No pretense, no posturing or politics, just simple and profound interaction with an unfettered heart. Such a heart engages the best places in me, places not visited nearly enough.

Such connection does not happen enough among us adults. To be childlike is to be open; knowing the safety of remaining closed pales in comparison to the reward of vulnerability. To be childlike is to be free--from opinions, ramifications, and the whiplash of the reaction. To be childlike is to be engaged. A child believes every situation is theirs and they can, and will, participate. And if the environment is too stale or "adult-like," get ready for a storm of open, free engagement.

Jocelyn Pence has taught me this about children and so much more. Her presence and posture of heart aims our own toward the best in people; most importantly, our children. She consistently reminds me of the deep wells of joy, hope, and strength running playfully all around us. Jocelyn's grace wipes away the adult fog from my eyes to see clearly the incredible wealth available in these precious ones we get to call our children.

I wholeheartedly encourage you to read *A Child Will Lead Them*. It will convict you as it has me. It will call forth the child in you and help you to adeptly engage the children around you. But I also urge you to take the next step: meet Jocelyn Pence. Reading this book is like someone telling you how great the food is but feeling incomplete because you haven't tasted it for yourself. I have the pleasure of being with Jocelyn just about whenever I want to. And trust me when I say this privilege is to encounter the Father's heart in a spiritual mom like few I've ever encountered. Meet her.

Be with children with her. Experience the honor, the awe, and the skill with which Jocelyn connects with children. You will be changed.

Many of you reading this book will never be able meet Jocelyn Pence. So, here is something every one of us can do to honor the heart of the Father in her: turn your heart to the children in your life. See them as God's gift to you. Be attentive to the heart and voice of the Lord reaching out to you through them. Allow their spirit to quicken your own, calling up the long-lost child within. That person is who you really are, the one whom God the Father thought about when He spoke you into your mother's womb. And that person sees children—and every person—as they really are.

Imagine a world such as this, a world filled with full-grown adults living open, free, and engaged. A world in which child-like adults live their lives as permission for all the other kids trapped inside adult bodies to run free. This is the world Jocelyn Pence dreams about and to which she devotes her life.

Join her.

Mark Durniak
Senior Pastor, World Harvest Outreach

ACKNOWLEDGMENTS

Chris Pence, my husband, my forever friend, my biggest fan: Your love for me has made me come alive again and again. You have, without hesitation, embraced every part of me. You are my strength, my resting place, and my very best friend. I love you more than words, and I love our life together.

Amberle, Rikka, and Carabelle, my three beautiful, strong daughters: You not only have taught me how to mother, but also how to be a child again. You truly are pillars in the family of God, and you are already changing the world with your incredibly powerful hearts. May you forever know that you are God's daughters, fully loved and delighted in by Him.

Mark Durniak, my pastor, my spiritual father, my brother, my friend: You have believed in me and have loved me enough to challenge me. You fearlessly call me to arise, all the while reminding me that I am, first and foremost, a beloved daughter of the Father. You made room for me to grow up freely into His heart and trusted the Lord in me. Thank you.

World Harvest Outreach, my loving, faithful, and fully present church family: You have trusted me, this vision, and this heart of the Father with your children. You have come all the way in with me, and the fruit has been beautiful and strong among us. I am so thankful. May His Person forever grow in us and in all of the children we receive together into our womb.

Diane Helman, my Jesus-sister, my first book editor, my friend: You have buried yourself in my heart. Having your hands edit this book has been a complete honor. Thank you for believing in and attributing value to this part of the Father's heart. It is what my every breath is for.

Brian Kisner, a faithful intercessor and dear friend to my husband and me: You saw Jesus in and upon me long ago, and you never stopped believing. Thank you.

ACKNOWLEDGMENTS

To my natural family who surrounds me, my husband, and our daughters: You have faithfully invested in us your love and support, your full belief, and your gentle guidance. You are such strength to us. I am forever thankful for each of you in my life. (Larry and Brenda Haugh, David and Catherine Pence, Larry and Shannon Yoder)

INTRODUCTION

Everything within me wants the whole world to know—deeply, fully, and transformatively—the heart of God for children. I pray that we would gather around the banqueting table of His heart for them, and taste and see how good He is.

But I know there are many who struggle to eat at this table of His heart for kids. I want to talk directly to these aching hearts so that we can all be unhindered and fully receptive to His thoughts.

The Lord says to you, "For unto you a child is born. A son has been given" (Isaiah 9:6).

For some of us, hearing the word *child* brings to the surface some things that need to be laid down. Painful memories resurface, dredging up reminders of a childhood that was far from perfect. Some experience fear or bitterness. Others carry deep disappointments because they can't conceive a child. Some feel failure when they hear the word *child*, instantly reminded of their inadequacies. These experiences affect us, and they cloud the ears by which we hear. If our childhood hurt us, we tend immediately to clam up so that we can only come in part of the way, subconsciously huddled in self-defense.

But if we truly want to hear our Father's heart for children, we must lay those things down and take up in exchange a refreshed and healed childlike hope. We refuse to carry those experiences into our future. In the Spirit, we take all these things and lay them down before His feet.

Jesus said,

> *"Whoever receives one child like this in My name receives Me; and whoever receives Me does not receive Me, but Him who sent Me"* (Mark 9:37b).

As we are seated here together around this table of God's heart, discussing His vision of children in the pages of this book, open your heart to receive them anew. Receive them in your spirit. See them. Let them get under your skin. Let's get into the Father's heart for them. We say together, "let the children come." Like Jesus, we will not forbid them. We let them come into our hearts. Let the children come.

PRAYER

Father, we want to hear Your heart. As purely as it comes out of Your heart, we want to receive it into our own.

We lay aside our wounds and come before You with an open heart and open spirit to hear. May our experiences, hurts, and failures not hinder us, or our children, from entering into all that You see. We don't want any walls in our hearts to hinder any child from entering into all that is in Your heart for them.

PART ONE

THE VISION

1

A MOMENT IN THE CITY OF GOD

I was in my kitchen, meditating on the Lord, when a piercing vision suddenly opened all around me. I saw children, boys and girls of all ages, running up and down the street. Some were dancing, some were playing, some were riding bicycles. They were the epitome of childlikeness. I could hear their voices in songs and laughter. As I watched, several little children rode their bicycles past an older gentleman who was in a wheelchair. They didn't say anything to him, but the man immediately got up, suddenly and fully healed.

Dumbfounded in my spirit, I stood motionless and transfixed, caught up entirely in what I had witnessed. "What am I seeing right now?" I asked the Lord. "What is this?!"

Then I saw another little child walk up to a convenience store, open the doors, and speak three or four words. Whatever he said was the word of the Lord for that place, and it responded immediately. When he came out of the building, the entire face of that business had changed.

As the vision faded, I looked at the Lord, eyes wide and heart afire. "Whatever it takes, and whatever I just saw, I am going to see this come to pass," I said. "I have to be a part of that opening up in children all over the earth!"

> "Thus says the LORD of hosts, 'Old men and old women will again sit in the streets of Jerusalem, each man with his staff in his hand because of age. And the streets of the city will be filled with boys and girls playing in its streets'" (Zechariah 8:4-5).

2

THE FATHER'S HEART FOR CHILDREN

A few years after my husband Chris and I were married, I felt a desire to get involved in the children's ministry at our church, so I offered myself to serve. I hung out with the kids during their class times, undeniably drawn to them. Each one was so unique and magnetic. I was mesmerized by them.

I began asking the children questions, such as, "If you could ask God any question—and you can!—what would it be?" or "What do you think God wants us to pray for the earth?"

Their thoughts and answers stunned me. They were thinking about things I had never thought of. They lived limitless. Boundary-less. I marveled at how their simple, childlike answers seemed to embody the purest Spirit of the Lord, full of the raw elements of faith, joy, and hope. The Lord started opening up their hearts to me, and the living breath of God in them filled me time and time again. I meditated in wonder on every word they spoke and every prayer they prayed. Their questions ignited something within me, and I was captivated.

Then, that day in my kitchen, the Lord opened my eyes. The vision I saw stopped me in my tracks. It entirely transformed the way I thought about children. It changed the way that I looked at Scripture. I found myself time and again undone in intercession for them. His heart had overcome me. I was completely addicted to what He sees in children.

Let's look anew, with open, renewable minds, at all that the Lord has to say about children and all that the Lord has entrusted to them. We will see them very differently. Absorbing His heart and vision for children will completely alter us and the way we walk with them.

Having the mind of Christ concerning children will cause an irreversible paradigm shift in us. We may once have thought of children as the church of the future, but now we will see that children are a vital and active part of the Body right now. We will become so convinced about our children that we will purposefully include them in all our endeavors. We will see that if we are not engaged with them, we are like a body walking around without a leg.

Let's call to mind some of the things Scripture has taught us about children.

Children are Our Example by Which to Enter the Kingdom

And He called a child to Himself and set him before them, and said, "Truly I say to you, unless you are converted and become like children, you will not enter the kingdom of heaven" (Matthew 18:2-3).

If we use our imagination, we can see a tremendous picture in Matthew when Jesus called the children to Himself. The disciples approached Jesus to contend for important seats in His Kingdom. *Who will be the greatest?* they asked, eager to know how to get to the top.

But Jesus calls a little child to Himself. Imagine Him drawing a skinny, mop-haired little boy close. This marks the only time in all of Scripture that Jesus places a human example before others in this way, by which to model themselves. He set a child before them.

Imagine the shockwaves that burst through all who heard this, as they processed these words from Jesus. *A child?* After spending their entire adult lives reaching for approval and importance (according to the religious or political leaders), they now see Jesus discard that system for an entirely different standard: that of a child.

Anyone can believe in Jesus for eternal life. But that is not maturity, and nor is it the Kingdom. Do you know how to enter the places of the Kingdom, how to walk in the places of maturity? You come as a child. You don't enter as a know-it-all. You don't even enter as a believer. You enter as a child.

Childlikeness is the access card to every heavenly realm. Every part of the Kingdom responds to the nature of a child. Jesus tells us that *"Whoever then humbles himself as this child is the greatest in the Kingdom of heaven* (Matthew 18:4).

Becoming like them is our entrance into the Kingdom.

Not only do we enter the Kingdom of Heaven as a child, but also our greatest influence is to be humble as a child.

Our Sons and Daughters Prophesy

*"'And it shall be in the last days,' God says, 'That I will pour forth of My Spirit on all mankind; And **your sons and your daughters***

shall prophesy, *And your young men shall see visions, And your old men shall dream dreams'"* (Acts 2:17).

Early one summer evening, 20 or 30 kids came together at church for a summer fun night before school resumed. We played water games, had snacks and laughed before coming together in a big circle to talk about Jesus.

In the middle of an activity, four-year-old McKinzee interrupted the group with a spontaneous announcement that seemed unrelated to our game. "There is someone who can't walk. Their back hurts. We have to pray for them. There is a baby in them."

The adults in the room blinked, surprised and unable to immediately discern what Kinzee was telling us. But because we have learned to trust the heart of the child, we took her comment in stride and trusted that it was Jesus speaking through her. We continued with our activity but acknowledged Kinzee's words, allowing them to hang in the air expectantly.

Within minutes, a senior couple from our congregation walked kindly into the kids' classroom. We invited them to join us in a project we had planned.

"I don't think we can," the husband declined, nodding to his wife beside him. "Susan hurt her back this morning and can hardly walk."

Instantly, Kinzee's words matched a current need, fueling our faith. Everyone in the room, kids young and grown, gathered around while young Kinzee laid her little hand on the back of our hurting friend. She prayed for her, and then we joined in.

When our prayers ended and Susan stood up, she rose without pain. Her eyes danced and my heart burst at her response: "I feel stronger! I feel like I could dance! I have never felt so much power and love in little ones!" She had been completely healed.

The Secrets of the Kingdom are Hidden in Children. They are Able to Teach Us with Wisdom.

*At that very time He rejoiced greatly in the Holy Spirit, and said, "I praise You, O Father, Lord of heaven and earth, that **You have hidden these things from the wise and intelligent and have revealed*** *them to infants. Yes, Father, for this way was well-pleasing in Your sight* (Luke 10:21).

*Then, after three days they found Him in the temple, sitting in the midst of the teachers, both listening to them and asking them questions. And **all who heard Him were amazed at His understanding and His answers*** (Luke 2:46-47).

One Sunday morning, all of our children were sitting together. My heart for the morning was leading me into teaching them about when Jesus was led by the Father into the wilderness for 40 days of fasting.

There are several common, key points we think of when we prepare to teach this story to children, but before I began, I wanted to hear from them. We hadn't even read the story yet.

I opened with the very beginning, simply saying that the Father led Jesus to the wilderness. God led Him there, not Satan. Jesus didn't get lost and end up in the wilderness. God His Father actually *led* Him to the wilderness. Why? Why would God lead Jesus to the wilderness?

The kids sat, pondering my question. A few of them offered answers that allowed me to see what each one was seeing with the Lord. One child said, "I see Jesus sitting on the side of a cliff, praying and talking to the Father."

"For sure," I agreed. "I think He did do a lot of praying while He was there. He probably talked to His Father a whole lot during that time."

Another child piped up. "I saw all these stars in the sky." I immediately knew in my spirit that the Holy Spirit was taking that child back to Abraham, and all the promises God had made to him. The Father was taking Jesus through this place, reminding Him of who He was and the promises that He had made for thousands of years. Promises that would be made a reality on Earth because of Him. I thought, *wow that's so cool.*

Then, quiet, six-year-old Emily raised her little hand and said, "I saw Jesus stepping from stone to stone, and I think it was God teaching Him how to lead."

I was completely awed. I could have just spent the whole day feasting on what was coming out of those kids. I knew it was the Lord talking to and through them.

There was a spirit of revelation on the children. They were reading between the lines, far past the basic, elementary-level lessons that we think of when it comes to that story. They actually put themselves into the Father's heart and asked Him questions, and He answered them clearly. He revealed the secrets of His heart, what He was doing with Jesus, and why that wilderness experience was so important.

I learned, and continue to learn, from them in this way. I went on to give them what I had in me to teach and invest in them, but I was so overtaken by the wisdom and the spirit of revelation that was on them. Those kids taught *me*. They brought the fullness of the Father's heart with the person of Jesus right into the room, and into me. They revealed to me a whole new understanding of that story. Their sight made that wilderness experience seem far more purposeful.

We can forever learn from them this way. Of course, we do not neglect our own teachings for them, but we see that together, we can learn a fuller picture of the heart of God in everything we teach or explore with them, in His Person and in Scripture.

If We Receive Children, We Receive Jesus

Taking a child, He set him before them, and taking him in His arms, He said to them, **"Whoever receives one child like this in My name receives Me..."** (Mark 9:36-37a).

Recently, I accepted an invitation to work at my daughters' public elementary school, filling in as needed. A week came when I was there a lot more than usual. I was spending time with many of the kids at the school. I became very familiar with them, learning that some of them came from home situations I could hardly comprehend.

I often come home exhausted after a day at the school. One evening, I was particularly exhausted, and I fell into bed at the earliest opportunity. Despite my deep sleep, I awoke in the middle of the night from a startling dream. I had been sitting around the table at the school with some of the kids that I knew came from really broken situations. I watched as they prophesied over me there in the middle of that school. The dream was incredibly intense, as real to me as my skin. The Lord had prophesied over my life, ministering to me not in a church or even in a Christian context, but through the spirit of children that don't even know Him. They were prophesying boldly to me! And I realized that I was receiving Him in those moments because I had received them: "Whoever receives one child like this in My name receives Me" (Mark 9:37a).

These words, offered to the disciples by Jesus, contain a simple yet profound promise. If I get Jesus when I receive a child, I want to receive every child. I want all of them because I want all of Him. I don't want just part of Him. I don't want Jesus in just my three children. I want Him in all of them, for with every child I receive, I get more of the Lord.

When we really believe this, we receive children with zeal. We will see things that we never saw in children before, and not just see, but receive.

The meaning of the original Greek word for "name" encompasses every aspect of all that we think or feel when a name is spoken or thought about. We can easily describe this as the "nature" of the person with the name. When I receive any one of them in His nature, in the way He loves and receives them, I receive Him.

Often, we only truly receive our own biological children. We see children in our community, and we think of them as someone else's child. Subconsciously, we categorize kids as "ours" and "not ours." But to receive the Lord in children, we must think differently. We must learn to see every one of them—on the street, at the park, everywhere we go—as our own. We receive them all. When we see them, we speak life over them. We love them. We laugh with them. We receive from their spirit as they run beside us in life.

We need our children. We need to be with them, and not just for their sake, but also for our own. We can learn from them and can hear the voice of the Father in them.

Children are Our Example in Faith, Love and Purity

*Let no one look down on your youthfulness, **but rather in speech, conduct, love, faith and purity, show yourself an example** of those who believe* (1 Timothy 4:12).

In 2 Kings 5, we see the influence of a little Israelite girl in the story of Naaman's healing from leprosy. The girl had been taken from her home by an enemy army and was made a servant of the warrior Naaman and his wife. Yet, when the little girl learned of Naaman's sickness, she set forth a remarkable example to us all. Though she had been taken captive from her homeland of Israel and enslaved, far from her family and her home, she still had a soft heart. She cared about her master's healing. When most would have resented this master, she cared for him. And so, she spoke up, guiding Naaman, through his wife, to the prophet of the Lord who could heal Naaman of his disease.

What incredible, unrestrained faith and such genuine, pure love—love for her enemy, even to desiring his healing. She truly cared for him. She did not become bitter and hard, even in such a horrible circumstance. Rather, she loved.

The heart of a child loves quickly, forgives quickly, and believes that there is goodness just around the corner. Children model a powerful example of genuine love, conduct, and purity. No one is without a second and third chance in the eyes of the childlike spirit. They truly are an example for us all.

A Child Will Lead Them

And the wolf will dwell with the lamb, And the leopard will lie down with the young goat, And the calf and the young lion and the fatling together; **And a little boy will lead them** (Isaiah 11:6).

Isaiah 11:1 prophesies, "Then a shoot will spring from the stem of Jesse…. Today we know that this prophecy refers to Jesus. The chapter continues by characterizing Jesus' rule as not that of an earthly king, but as one of compassion, righteousness, justice, and faithfulness, and of seeing and hearing the hearts of men.

Isaiah then begins to describe the culture that would come from His rule, saying in verse 6: "…And a little boy will lead them." The culture of Jesus is a place where even a child can lead. In verses 8-9a, we read, "The nursing child will play by the whole of the cobra, And the weaned child will put his hand on the viper's den. They will not hurt or destroy in all my holy mountain…" Recall with me the time when Jesus addressed the Pharisees as, "You serpents, you brood of vipers…" (Matthew 23:33). This helps us understand what Isaiah was referring to: a time when the Pharisaical system, the religious system of Jesus' day, would no longer bite or poison the childlike spirit.

Jesus establishes a culture where a childlike spirit will lead. His rule is one where a child can play, imagine, and explore without the fear-driven constraints of a religious system. The childlike spirit is holy, pure, and brand new, full of faith and possibility. Jesus' ways safeguard them from being poisoned or limited by a system of religion or rigid arguments of doctrine.

Everything within me cries out, "Hallelujah! Praise the Lord! For the culture of Jesus sets our children free!" They are free to lead us, and to imagine, dream, and believe.

We see that in His Kingdom, it is safe for a child to lead. Not only is it safe, but I would submit to you that if you feel called to lead, then you are called to become like a child. Remember again Jesus' words in Matthew 18:3, "… unless you are converted and become like children…" If I feel called to lead, I am called to be as a child. I am to live as a child of God, whose love is full and strong and forgiving. Whose imagination and faith are limitless. Whose sight is pure. Whose trust is not withheld. Whose heart remains tender and soft and believing. This is how we lead.

Yes, the child will grow in wisdom and stature. We see that in Scripture. It tells us that the child Jesus grew in wisdom and stature. The child Samuel grew in favor with God and with man. But in each of these, notice that the *child grew*. They didn't lose or lay aside that beautiful, pure person that was introduced into this world.

Our Children are Miraculous Wonders

Behold, **I and the children whom the LORD has given me are for signs and wonders** *in Israel from the LORD of hosts, who dwells on Mount Zion* (Isaiah 8:18).

Have you ever encountered the ministry of children?

My girls and I often visit a low-income neighborhood across town. I don't like going there if I don't have my kids with me. I have built relationships with many families in that community, and if my girls aren't able to come along, I immediately seek out those children when I arrive. The faith of those children, even from unbelieving broken families, is unspeakably empowering and fruitful.

The miracles we have seen in that place are amazing. One day, a group of us were knocking on doors in the community, inviting children to join us for a neighborhood balloon party. We collected kids as we went; at each home, the group of excited, giggling children grew larger. At one home, the green door swung open slowly. The man inside stared at us hesitantly and offered no greeting. As we extended our cheery invitation, the kids could see a little girl sitting on the coffee table as they peered through the door. Other children played nearby. The kids began to love on him, telling him, "You're a good dad. We love you. You should bring your kids to our balloon party. Do you know that Jesus loves you?"

They didn't know he had just kidnapped a child. The little girl was his daughter, but he had refused to return her to her mother for several days. We left after a few moments and went to our balloon party. A little later, a mother from another home in that community came down the hill crying, pushing a stroller with the same little girl in the front. "I don't know what you guys did, but he gave me my baby girl back! He gave me my baby back!"

Within minutes of encountering our children, this man had called the mother of the kidnapped child and returned her to her mother, of his own free will, after days of refusal. Now that is a miraculous wonder. That is the miracle of a heart changed.

Children are Kings and Queens

Jehoash was seven years old when he became king (2 Kings 11:21).

Jehoash became ruler at a very difficult time in Israel's history. He was seated as king just after all the Baal prophets had been destroyed. He was only seven years old. Can you see a seven-year-old as a king? We look at seven-year-olds and think they're ready to color a unicorn, play at the park, or go to school so they can learn about life for the next 13 years. But the Father calls them up to rule entire atmospheres! They are kings and queens in the Spirit. As parents, we are to call up and train their sight and voice. We take them into places like the grocery store and we ask them, "What is something you want to establish for this atmosphere? What atmosphere are we creating for the people here? We're coming in here and there are broken people in this store."

Our children can establish an atmosphere for the people in every place they go. They can rule. It's powerful when a child walks up to a lady in the cereal aisle and thanks her for something about who she is, or when a gentle child offers something encouraging to a furrowed old man in his wheelchair. No one rejects a child's soft "I love you." No matter what the child says, that person will not forget it. What's more, the spirit that is released through the child will follow that person.

Surely goodness and lovingkindness will follow me... (Psalm 23:6a).

When my oldest was entering kindergarten, I knew I had a very short period of time to teach her how to walk as a daughter who has authority in her school, as a queen who could establish an atmosphere wherever she goes. In our school district, kindergarten parents are able to walk their students to the kindergarten classroom for the first three days of school. After that, you drop your child off at the door. I knew those three days were my opportunity to teach her how to establish an atmosphere in that place. She was 5 years old, going into public school for the first time. Every morning for those three days (and every day since), we walked to school together. The trip was only a short walk and each time, I would say, "Amber, what do you want for your school today from your heart?"

On the very first morning, she said, "I want them to have the fruit of the Spirit." I nodded in agreement as we crossed the threshold into the school, and lowered myself to walk right beside her, whispering in her ear.

"Okay," I said, "This is how we're going to pray. With every footstep, we're going to say another fruit of the Spirit. Jesus said any place our feet travel is our place to influence. It's our territory. So, with every step we take to your classroom, we're going to believe Him. You and I are going to whisper "love, joy, peace, patience…""

And we did. We repeated the fruit of the Spirit the entire way to her kindergarten classroom. We did this all three mornings. We walked down the halls together and spoke over what she wanted to give her school, her teachers, and her classmates. This is how I was teaching her how to create an atmosphere, how to walk as a queen of the Lord.

As her kindergarten year continued, I would walk to school to pick her up at the end of each day. I would always ask, "Amber, did you see Jesus at school today?"

About a week into school, she said, "Yes, Mommy! I saw Jesus at school today!"

"Well, what did He look like?" I asked. "Where was He? Did He say anything?"

"He came over, knelt down, and put His hands on my feet, and I heard Him praying for me," she answered clearly. "Then He got up, hugged me, kissed me on the head, and walked away."

In those moments, the Lord ministered faith to my mothering heart. He was reassuring me that He was taking care of my firstborn child at school. But also, even more than that, I realized that Amber, in the middle of a public school of over 900 students, had established an atmosphere of Heaven. The literal person of Jesus walked in the room and she recognized, saw, felt, and heard Him praying for her, touching her feet, hugging her, kissing her head. She knew He was there. She brought an awareness of Jesus Himself, our Emmanuel, just by walking through the school and learning and practicing that she gets to say what goes. She gets to choose what atmosphere reigns there. She gets to give of her heart to every single one in that school.

When our children establish this kind of atmosphere, many others will also encounter the person of Jesus.

Our Children are Filled with the Holy Spirit from the Womb for Us

When Elizabeth heard Mary's greeting, **the baby leaped in her womb; and Elizabeth was filled with the Holy Spirit** (Luke 1:41).

John the Baptist, in his mother's belly, was filled with the Holy Spirit. You do not need to go to the altar and have someone pray over you if you want to be filled with the Holy Spirit. John was in the belly. He didn't even know how to ask for it yet, and he was filled to a point that when he jumped in his mother's belly, *she* was filled.

He leaped; Elizabeth was filled. This presence and filling of the Holy Spirit is in our babies! Jesus, may we receive them! Even now, pause for a moment and tell the Lord, "I receive them. I want to receive every bit of this, of them."

When my youngest daughter Cara was in my belly, the Lord specifically told me that she would be my Joseph. She would be a dreamer. He also told me that she would open my heart and the hearts of others to see the atmosphere of Heaven around them, and even angels. She released these things in me. Not long after He spoke these things to me, I began to have dreams like I had never had before. I also had several encounters where I knew I was seeing and experiencing the care of an angel.

Once, while still pregnant with Cara, I was caring for my other two toddler daughters (all three of my children are extremely close in age) and I was exhausted. I had heroically managed to get my daughters to nap at the same time that day, which any mother of little ones knows is a huge feat. Grabbing my opportunity for a rest, I lay down. In the middle of a deep sleep, I woke up and saw two huge feet beside me. They were pointed towards my body, but then they turned, and I watched them walk away. I knew they were the feet of an angel that had been ministering to my physical body, ministering strength and rest while I was sleeping.

This is something Cara released into me before I could ever even hold her, like John the Baptist. When he jumped in his mother's belly, he released the Holy Spirit in her. Elizabeth was filled with the Holy Spirit because of John. That is Cara. She released things in me before I could ever look into her eyes, before she could ever say a word or lay a hand on me to pray for me. Her simple presence in my belly released me into an awareness of the Lord in my dreams, and an awareness of the atmosphere of Heaven around me.

Not only are our children filled with the Spirit in the womb, but they are also *called*.

Our Children are Called from the Womb

Cara continues to manifest these things as she grows. When she was four years old, three people contacted me over a year's time, saying that Cara had visited them in a dream, praying over them. One even commented that he awoke from the dream in the power of God. I realized she was living out what the Lord had told me about her when she was in my womb.

But when God, who had set me apart even from my mother's womb and called me through His grace... (Galatians 1:15).

Before I formed you in the womb I knew you, And before you were born I consecrated you... (Jeremiah 1:5a).

It doesn't matter whether your kids are yet seeing what you're seeing in their lives. They are called from the womb with a purpose. God has filled our children with His Spirit.

In Judges 13, we see that the angel of the Lord came to Samson's mother before she was even pregnant, telling her she would have a son and that he would be a Nazarite (holy, consecrated to the Lord) from the womb. He instructed her to walk as a Nazarite while her baby was still in her belly. She had to walk with Samson, as a Nazarite. She walked with him in his identity from the time he was called, even while he was in her womb.

From the Mouths of Children, He Establishes His Strength. From Their Mouths Comes Prepared Praise.

...and said to Him, "Do You hear what these children are saying?" And Jesus said to them, "Yes; have you never read, 'Out of the mouth of infants and nursing babies You have prepared praise for Yourself'?" (Matthew 21:16)

Matthew 21 paints a picture of chaos. After Jesus triumphantly enters Jerusalem on the back of the donkey, surrounded by waving palm branches and shouts of "Hosanna!" He goes into the temple. There He finds a holy place that has become a marketplace. Enterprising men have made a business out of the law. Jesus zealously overturns their bartering tables. Now there's a huge mess of tumbling coins, angry merchants, and scattering animals. Simultaneously, blind and lame people are coming to Jesus in search of healing. This is truly a crazy moment. But on top of all this, Matthew describes children running around in the temple, shouting. They are not sitting softly or reverently, with their little hands folded together. No, it says they were shouting, "Hosanna to the Son of David!" (Matthew 21:15b).

This was the tipping point for the scribes and the priests, which prompted their indignant question to Jesus. You would think they would be upset because of all the other chaos happening in the temple at that moment, but no, it was the shouts of praise from the children that angered them. In that moment, those children were declaring the word of the Lord. It was a prophetic sound. The children saw the Lord when the scribes and Pharisees were unable to see Him, and it pricked their hearts.

This is in our children. They see Jesus. They recognize Him. They can see in the Spirit and they're not afraid to speak it, especially when you can't see it.

Jesus offered the temple officials an astounding response. "Have you never read, '*Out of the mouth of infants and nursing babes You have prepared praise for Yourself*'?"

Prepared praise. It's not just happenstance. There are songs that have already been written in the heavenlies that the Lord, on purpose and by divine design, prepared your child to carry. Jesus' words are quoted from Psalm 8:2, where the original Hebrew reads, "*from the mouth of infant and nursing babes you have established strength Because of your adversaries...*" God gives us children to be strength to us *because* of the season or adversities that we face. I often hear mothers complaining, "Oh I don't know, I just already have this trouble at work, and then I come home, and I got this baby crying and..." But the Lord is saying, "I gave that child to you because in him is your strength! That's what's going to get you through this. But you are wallowing in complaints toward your children, and you are consumed by making them convenient or quiet!"

Let those who have ears to hear, let them hear! Children are our strength in the midst of our adversity. They are not merely a sweet experience on a sunny day when everyone's playing and happy. They are our strength when we are attacked and when life feels hard or dark. *From the mouth of infants and nursing babes You have established strength*. We need nursing babies in our lives. We all do. In them is our strength.

May we learn to welcome the running, boisterous kids that are shouting the word of the Lord. God forbid that I be distracted by them. The modern church has created separate spaces for children where they are rarely able to participate in what their parents are doing. We fear that children will be a distraction to our carefully-crafted services. It grieves the Father's heart that anyone would dare to consider children a distraction in worship. God forbid I ever be distracted by them. God forbid that I feel like that little tap on my leg is going to take me out the presence of God. No, a child's heart will take us into the presence of God! Out of their mouths is praise, and it's been prepared in the heavenlies for all the world to hear. God Himself has placed this in them to be released. I want to hear it.

One Sunday during our worship time, a little girl named Lorelei was sitting near me. I leaned over and asked, "What song do you hear the Lord singing right now?"

She looked at me and said, "All I keep saying is the ground is holy. The ground is holy." In her hands was a piece of paper on which she had written over and over, "The ground is holy. The ground is holy."

Immediately, I felt like I was Moses on holy ground, and I slipped out of my shoes. There was a prepared song in her that I needed to hear and join with. We need them in worship with us because they carry the timely, prepared praise of the Lord. What's more, the atmosphere of children can help adults enter into God's Presence. Many times, adults go into worship carrying large amounts of baggage. It can take a long time for us to wade through it all so we can see the Lord.

But our children do not struggle with this. Kids live in the Spirit, moving in and out without complication. They refuse to hold onto baggage and offense and disappointment. They don't have to lay all that stuff down every time we gather, so it doesn't take them near the amount of time it takes us to enter into the place where we can see and experience Him. They see Him instantly. They are with Him, and if we allow them, will carry us right into His Presence.

Children Know the Father and Can Deeply Encounter His Presence

I have written to you, children, because you know the Father (1 John 2:13c).

One Sunday, all the church kids and I were in worship with the adult believers. As the whole church gathered together, a wave of the Spirit came over everyone. People were sitting or lying on the floor, caught up in personal encounters with the Lord. Several of our children experienced this time as well. They were piled in a small huddle, weeping on each other as they each had personal encounters. Some of them could not talk because they were weeping so hard. During that time, the Lord visited each of them. Some saw how the Lord had created them. One little girl saw moments that happened in Heaven before she was born. Others who had more painful backgrounds in their young years experienced the direct voice of the Lord, who was healing things in their hearts that no one else could touch or heal.

Children know the Father. The global church has been talking a lot in recent years about fathering. We're learning how to be fathered by the Lord. Our example for this is in children. They know the Father, simply, purely and deeply.

Another day, as we were sitting in a circle in class, one of the kids began to share. She was a little girl, and her precious heart opened up about being really scared of her family's home not being heated, and the weight her parents were carrying to provide heat in their home due to financial strain. Everyone sat quietly as she shared; you could feel the genuine sincerity in her dear heart.

After a few moments of silence, I looked at the children in the circle. "Don't be afraid to do what's happening in your heart."

One of the children got up and laid her hand on her fearful friend. Another walked over, took her friend's hands in her own, looked straight into her eyes and delivered a personal message so holy and beautiful that no one could move. That day, the children effectively ministered to deep places of the heart.

Our Children Carry Bread for the Whole

One of His disciples, Andrew, Simon Peter's brother, said to Him, "There is a lad here who has five barley loaves and two fish…" (John 6:8-9a)

Children are for all of us, the whole Body. I think of the little boy who had the bread and fish that fed 5,000 people. The scriptural account of that story reveals that before they found the little boy and his food, Jesus already knew how He was going to feed them. But the disciples didn't know that. Jesus looked at the people, and then to the disciples, saying, "I want to feed them." To test one of His disciples, He asked, "How are we going to do this?" Jesus already had a plan. He knew that there was a child for the whole. There's a child with something that would fill the whole. Andrew was the disciple that found the little boy and brought him right to Jesus.

One Sunday morning, we had an unusually wide range of ages in the same kids' class. We had been doing a series of classes on the different kinds of gifts we find in Scripture. We were talking about the gifts or treasures of wisdom in Proverbs. We talked about the gifts of God that are on the inside of us for our world, and about the gift of Jesus given to us. On this particular morning, we discussed the gift of our heart, and that we give all of who we are to God in an intimate exchange. I asked the kids to imagine giving a gift of themselves, something from within themselves that they wanted to give to the Lord. After a few moments of imagination in which they privately presented their gift to Jesus, I asked them to tell me how He had received their gift. What was His response? What did He look like? What did He do? We went around the room, giving each child an opportunity to share if they wanted to. It was clear that the kids were having beautiful experiences with the Lord, giving specific parts of who they are back to Him.

We came to little three-year-old Oliver. "What did you see?" I asked.

"I saw God," he answered simply, with a heaviness.

Gently, I coaxed him. "Well, what did He look like? Was He happy? Was He sad?"

His reply was immediate. "He was mad."

Of course, I wanted to quickly reassure him that God wasn't mad at him. God is happy. He loves us.

But I knew that I needed to ask Oliver to explain what he was experiencing, so I decided to dig a little deeper.

"Why do you think He was mad?"

The dear little boy looked right into my eyes. "He's mad because we won't open His gifts to us."

Immediately, the weight of the Lord was in the room. Everyone could feel it. What this little boy was experiencing with Jesus was real, and his words carried weight for our entire church family. He opened up something from the Father's heart that we needed to hear. And the Lord trusted this three-year-old with a message that was for all, young and old.

Children all around us are carrying these kinds of messages, timely messages, straight from the heart of God. They are ours, and they are for us. May we receive them as our own.

> *"Lift up your eyes and look around; all your children gather and come to you. As surely as I live," declares the LORD, "you will wear them all as ornaments; you will put them on, like a bride"* (Isaiah 49:18 NIV).

In this Scripture, the Lord wasn't looking at one mother and telling her to gather her personal brood of children. He was calling all of Israel: "Look at all your children. They're coming to you. See them. You have children. All of you. Receive them!"

I urge you in this same way, that you see the children all around you and receive them.

PART TWO

THE FOUNDATION LAID IN US

3

THE CHILDLIKE SPIRIT

If we return to Matthew 18:2, when Jesus set the boy before the disciples as a model for Kingdom greatness, He says, "unless you are **converted** and become like children..." The Greek word for "converted" means that everything changes. You turn and go back. You go a completely different direction. Your mindset changes. Literally, everything changes. My entire thinking and entire paradigm for life transforms. It is not enough to strap a childlike idea onto the Jesus we already have experienced. Rather, becoming like a child is a process that restores and transforms us. It changes the entire manner by which we think, the way that we approach Him, and the way we relate to one another.

Jesus purposefully offers us the example of a child's heart as the manner by which we experience this transformation. If we tried to do this in our adult skins, many of us would struggle indefinitely. We might immediately start striving to become what He says we already are. If we were the ones set before another, we might experience feelings of inadequacy or self-conscious comparison. We might begin to feel as though all eyes are on us, prompting us to fuss: "How should I sit? How should I receive? They are all watching me. Should I put my makeup on? Should I smile or look somber?" We would become preoccupied by details that children have no regard for.

It had to be a child. A child's simple, unimpeachable openness and curiosity discards all our useless concerns. Jesus invites us as children for a deep and precious reason: the childlike spirit doesn't strive to become what he already is. There is rest and freedom in the spirit of a child.

What is Childlikeness?

If I was to describe childlikeness in the simplest way, it would be **brand new.** Childlikeness is brand-newness. I did a search of

Scripture once, to find out what "child" means in its Hebrew and Greek definitions. What I found was powerfully simple. *Child* refers to a brand-new person in every scope: physically, mentally, spiritually. When my heart becomes childlike, my ability to trust is restored. Hope reappears in my imagination. Love and forgiveness flow freely.

We know that when we are frustrated or short-tempered with our children, they still come quickly back to our feet. Children keep no record of our mistakes. They easily live with a fresh slate. *Brand new.*

Children Come

"Let the little children come to me...." (Matthew 19:14a NIV)

Put simply, children come. They just *come*. Orphans run, but children come. It's like when my husband comes home, and our children run to him, calling out "Daddy!" He doesn't have to coerce them. They simply and gladly come. That's what happens in Mark 10, where Jesus is with the disciples, and many people are bringing their children to Him. The disciples try to block the children, until Jesus says, "Let the little children come to me"! Children don't have a problem coming. They simply come. It's natural for them.

In the parable of the prodigal son, the father had to patiently wait, allowing his son to get to a condition where he would *decide* to come home. The father did not go out and drag him home by his ear. He allowed a process to happen in his son's life that changed his heart back to that of a child who would come to him.

The Heart of Mankind is Childlike

One April evening, I stepped onto my back porch, which is one of my favorite places to be with the Lord. My kids had gone to bed and my husband was seeing a movie with friends, so I had a couple of hours to myself where I could be with Him. I was eager for some Jesus time, but had nothing specific in mind except to be with Him. But within moments, He was showing me the heart of man. I was overtaken by the childlike richness in the heart of man. I began to weep.

The original heart of man is open, embracing everything in life. The mind will try to shut out trauma, but the heart of man doesn't shut it out. It's teeming with raw, pure light. Even in pain, it is full of purity, belief, hope and love—overcoming every evil substance. The inward heart of man is childlike. Instantly, I realized that I don't ever want to be disconnected from that heart in me. Ever. I refuse to be cut off from that depth of tenderness.

The Father calls us "children of God" for a reason. We are sons and daughters. We are His children. Jesus Himself says, "I am the Son of God." He never loses the childlikeness in His care for us. Scripture says that His mercies are new every morning. Oh, to sit in that for a minute. *His mercies are new.* Every morning, brand new. That is childlike.

Immediately, I was reminded of a lady I met while on a ministry trip to Costa Rica. I had been speaking to a group of ministry leaders about children and the Father's heart for them, and she came to me afterward, weeping. Through her sobs, she began to share that she had been badly abused and had no memory of her childhood. Her mind had shut out an entire portion of her life. Yet, when I was with her, all I could see was her beautiful childlike heart, so open and raw and pure. Her heart had not forgotten its original, childlike self, even as her mind had erased her childhood.

I held this memory closely in my spirit as the Lord opened my eyes. I saw this beautiful childlike heart everywhere, even in people who cannot remember or appreciate any part of their childhood; even in those who appear to be hard or lost in their sin; even in those doing the works of evil. Every living person has a childlike heart, even after their minds have been trained in survival. Even after their hearts have been built up with walls so that nothing can penetrate. I could see that heart underneath all of it. Their hearts still long for connection and still have the capacity to hurt. Underneath the layers is a heart that is tender and open and raw and pure and childlike. If only they would allow their walls to crumble, revealing this beautiful beating miracle that the Lord formed on the inside of them.

There is a child on the inside of every one of us that does not want to be forsaken. Our heart wants us to be fully connected with it. We are always meant to be children. There is never a time that we are not meant to see God as our Father and relate to Him as His son or daughter, a child whom He loves and has always loved.

Children are far greater than we often realize and are far more important than perhaps we were encouraged to believe we were when we were young. In Matthew 19, mothers began bringing their children to Jesus in the hope that He would touch them and bless them. But the disciples found the children bothersome and shielded Jesus from the kids. Some translations even say they were shooing them away! But Scripture tells us that Jesus became indignant about this. In His response, His love for and value of children was plainly revealed:

> *Let the children alone, and do not hinder them from coming to Me; for the kingdom of heaven belongs to such as these* (Matthew 19:14).

I submit to you that not only is Jesus pleading with us to allow the children to come to Him, but He is also calling deeply to the child within each of us.

Many times, we shoo that child away.

It grieves me how often we literally push our own childlike spirits to the side. We believe our words to be too simple, or that no one will want to hear them. Maybe we ache because we weren't received when we were children, so we flinch from fears of further rejection. When we adopt these things into us, we miss doors of entry into the Kingdom. When something from our childlike spirit arises in us, we suppress it. We shoo away our own childlikeness, like the disciples did with the children, wrongfully silencing the powerful simplicity of the Lord in us. We come to Him with all of our knowledge, our accumulated experience, and our maturity, forgetting that He calls us His children.

He actually delights in us as His children. The childlike spirit He authored in us is tender, loving, forgiving, and believing. This draws us with affection and joy into His depths. By posturing ourselves before Him as adults, we miss the re-ignition of an imagination that is pure, limitless, and untainted by disappointment, pain, and darkness.

Jesus does not want us to put childlikeness away. He desires childlike hearts and spirits. When we remember how teachable and believing children are, it is easy to see why He would long for us to come to Him that way. Brand new. Wide open. Full of wonder.

Full of faith. We must not put away, lose, run from, or devalue the childlike spirit we have. It is an important part of who we are.

One evening as I was studying this more deeply, the Lord sent a timely, confirming word through my daughter Rikka. She came into the room with two little keys that appeared to belong to some luggage. She held them up to me, saying, "Mommy, these keys are yours. They will open all the doors. All the doors, Mommy." Her blue eyes held mine earnestly, with complete belief. Then she added a final thought, "and they open all the oils!" Then she dropped the keys in my hands and ran off to play.

I sat there with the Lord, speechless. Tears rolled down my face, and I let her words seep into my spirit, fully receiving the heart of the Father through Rikka. I realized that in that moment, the Lord was fully emphasizing the weight and importance of what I was learning. He has given us the keys to the childlike spirit. It opens doors that no one else can open. He is giving us all the keys to all the doors, and to the anointing of the Lord. The balm of Gilead, healing oils, the oil of gladness.

Do you see how tapped-in our kids are? I sat there, clutching those keys in my hands. All I could say to the Lord, over and over, was "Thank you. Thank You, Papa. You are so good to us."

I am convinced there are doors that only a child can open.

Moses: A Baby with a Key

One example of this is the early life of Moses. The Lord began the deliverance of Israel—an entire nation—by placing a child in Pharaoh's house. Imagine what might have been the result if the Lord had sent an adult Hebrew slave. Likely, they probably would have cried, "Away with him!" and sent him to be done away with or to be punished.

But, brilliantly, the Lord sent a baby. Pharaoh's daughter couldn't resist the child. This was a door into Pharaoh's house that only a child could open. Because of this, Moses grew up with the bearing and posture of royalty, and it had to happen that way. Slaves can't lead slaves to freedom.

Some things do not happen, and some things are not open, without a childlike spirit to access them.

Abimelech and Abraham

During the time the Lord was teaching me about the heart of man, I was doing some personal study of Genesis, and became caught up in the story of Abraham and Sarah. Abraham had a history of lying about Sarah, his wife, by referring to her as his sister. He had first done this when he was still Abram and she was Sarai. But sometime later, after their names had been changed to Abraham and Sarah, and after the Lord had made a covenant with them, Abraham repeated this behavior.

They were traveling through a land and came upon the king of that land, Abimelech. As they prepared to sojourn in this land, Abraham gave Sarah clear instructions: if anybody asks who you are, tell them that you're my sister. Do not tell them that you're my wife. When they appeared before King Abimelech, Abraham asked for permission to sojourn in his land. In the course of their meeting, Abimelech asked Sarah to go home with him. Abraham said yes, because she was just his sister.

That night, the Lord spoke to Abimelech in a stern warning, saying, "Don't you dare touch her. This is Abraham's wife." And so, Abimelech did not touch her, and was sorry he had taken her. He hadn't realized his mistake. The next day, Abimelech went to Abraham, demanding to know why he had lied. "Why did you tell me she was your sister? Your God told me not to dare touch her!" Understandably, Abimelech was angry.

Abraham responded by admitting he had been afraid. "I was afraid that you would do something to me if I didn't let you have her, and so I lied." In an effort to make things right, Abimelech brought animals to Abraham and returned Sarah, untouched.

At the end of that story, Scripture says that Abraham prayed for Abimelech, because, when Abimelech took Sarah, the Lord had closed all the wombs in the entire royal family and royal household. Servants, concubines, wives; no one was able to bear children because of Abimelech's mistake. But when Abraham prayed for Abimelech, the Lord opened all the wombs for Abimelech's house to bear children again.

As I read this story, I felt badly for Abimelech, who had been graciously allowing Abraham to sojourn in his land, and had no idea he was doing anything wrong by taking Sarah into his house. Yet, all of a sudden, he could not have children. His whole house was locked up and his legacy cut off. It felt harsh, considering that the moment the Lord warned him not to touch her, he immediately obeyed.

As I sat there feeling sorry for Abimelech, I heard the audible voice of the Lord. He said, "You are no longer childless." Immediately in my heart, I began to see more than just this story. I saw that there are many people who have been battered by life, and not even necessarily by things they had any control over. Those experiences have hardened their hearts or have taken their childlikeness from them. Their ability to trust, believe, or hope has been cut off.

The Lord was speaking directly of those that have been tumbled by life, whose inner childlike heart seems so far from them. They feel no ability to have a childlike heart, with its legacy of faith and trust and love. He said, "Now. Now is the time. You are no longer childless. There is a child in you. You can connect to that childlike heart again." In these moments, the Lord was not just speaking to a womb. I heard him saying to men's and women's hearts, "You will no longer be disconnected from childlikeness."

Life happens. Sometimes we make bad choices in life. Abimelech honestly didn't intend to get himself into a bad situation, but the consequences detached him from having children. When trouble happens in life, our brains try to shut it out. These survival mechanisms disconnect us from childlikeness. In Ezekiel 11:19 the Lord said that He would remove our heart of stone and give us a heart of flesh! This is about our hearts and staying ever connected to that childlike tenderness and openness.

I'm sure that many of you reading this struggle with a sense of loss, as though you have no idea how to restore your own childlike spirit. You have been hurt, and so much life has happened. The Lord's thoughts pierce straight through those concerns. I hear His voice saying to you, "You are no longer childless. You have that childlikeness. It is still in you. You are not childless. You have always been My child. Your heart is fashioned after Mine. If you'll do this with Me, it can be for you."

Whenever we feel like we cannot connect to the brand-newness of a childlike spirit, we prophesy by faith over our hearts before the Lord. We can say, "I am not childless. I am brand new, right here." You are not childless, even when you feel like you cannot connect to the pure, innocent love within. He says you can. Sit with Him and let Him love you as a Father and let Him free you to be a child again.

It is not only men and women who struggle with this. Do you know there are physical children in our communities and all over the world who no longer know this childlikeness within themselves anymore? Every day we encounter children who no longer hear their childlike spirit. Too much life has happened. It can break your heart. There are many of them for whom life has already tumbled over. The consequences of decisions in their home have made a severe mark. The light of a childlike spirit has been extinguished from their eyes.

How I desire the heart of every person to know that it is childlike. I want the heart of children to remain forever brand new.

Solomon

In Ecclesiastes 11, Solomon, the wisest man who ever lived, gives us many pieces of wisdom and advice. He encourages us to sow our seed and to enjoy youth while we have it. He tells us to rejoice in our childhood. At the end of chapter 11, in verse 10, he writes:

"...so remove grief and anger from your heart and put away pain from your body, because childhood and the prime of life are fleeting."

I hear a father pleading with his son to cherish his childlikeness, because it is fleeting. It's like a breath. It can so quickly be snuffed out by bitterness and anger as you walk through experiences in life and relationships. It is so easy for a single offense or negative experience to cause us to throw walls up. Thus, our hearts become hard and closed because of our pain.

But I hear Solomon pleading with our spirits to strip that stuff off. Strip anger and bitterness away from you. Cherish the innocence that loves purely. Hold fast to love that trusts, forgives, is not skeptical, and does not bring rash judgments. Think of a child. They are resilient in love. I think of my own daughters. When I mess up, they forgive me and run to me immediately. The walls don't go up. In the same way, Solomon pleads with our hearts because so easily, so very quickly, the childlikeness in our hearts can be snuffed out. This is similar to guarding our hearts; we must continually allow for healing where there is pain and remove the bitterness that can settle in after offenses. The childlikeness of our hearts is to be cherished and guarded, remaining open and tender.

Children do this readily and we can relearn it from them.

Be Childlike Again

Though children are often primary on my personal radar, it is in the heart for all men to be childlike and to know their Papa. Many people we encounter were parented in families that don't know Papa, and we have the unique opportunity to be a father or mother to them. We have the open door to love and guide and be with them, not only our own, but also those children who are around us whose parents cannot teach them and relate to them this way. A lot of children come to my house to play with my kids, and they come without parents. Every opportunity to love them as my own and to connect with them in that way is invaluable.

A little girl named Reyna from our community wanted to come along to church with me, so my family and I picked her up and brought her with us. Reyna came to us from an impoverished and broken family background. She loved having our church van pick her up and bring her to church. She began absorbing everything she could about Jesus' love for her. Her heart was wide open. Anytime she came, she was attached to my hip.

One Sunday, we were sitting together, and she noticed the anointing oil perched on a speaker on the stage. She tipped her face to mine and asked why the oil was there.

Leaning over, I said, "It is called anointing oil. Jesus anoints us with His heart, His Spirit, and His presence. So, when we anoint someone, we put oil on them as a picture of what Jesus does to us. When He anoints us, it's like He smears the oil of His presence on us, and then we get all shiny in Jesus!"

Her eyes were gleaming with light, as big as saucers. Her heart was perfectly childlike, ready to receive and believe. The worship music continued, and after a few moments passed, I looked at her and asked, "Do you want me to anoint you?"

It was as though I had offered her a block of gold. Her whole countenance came alive and shone with belief and desire. "Yes!" she squealed in a half whisper.

"You can be anointed anytime, not just on special occasions," I told her. "He anoints us when we are in His presence, smearing us with Himself."

It was a privilege to anoint Reyna that day. It was one of the most simple and beautiful moments that my heart has ever experienced. Her spirit was purely childlike. Even though she had already lived a hard life, and at such a young age, her heart remained childlike, beautifully open and tender and believing.

Doesn't Reyna make you want to be like a child in your heart again?

I forever want this kind of wonder and tenderness in my heart. Every day I want to be brand new and childlike, with no arguments in a mind of unworthiness. No voice of accusation. No spirit of disappointment. Just brand new. We can live in perfect trust that if He said this is for me, it is for me.

Some of you, though, don't know if your heart can handle being childlike again. The pain of broken childhoods can be hard to bear. It can leave such a residue in our hearts that makes tenderness, openness, and trust feel like a foolish risk. But this is the invitation of the Lord for you to be childlike again. We are His children, and the genuine heart that He gave us is childlike.

Spend Time with Children

I have found that the best way for me to become as a child is to spend time with children. I humble myself to learn from them and allow their pure spirit to wash my own. I witness their love, resilience, and forgiveness. I am reborn when I listen to how they think, imagine, and believe. I relearn trust. The purity in their hearts challenges my judgments. Their wonder heals my cynicism. Soon I discover myself becoming like them. I find my heart freer to imagine, to dream, to trust, to forgive. I ask them questions and am taught by the Lord in them. Becoming like them is a beautiful unraveling of my heart before my Father, as I learn of Him, as *His* child. Oh, the wonder of forever being His child!

Let us never forget that inside all of us is a childlike spirit. It never ages or expires, even as our minds adopt adult thinking. Childlikeness is how we best connect with one another. The best way to connect with people who seem resistant to us isn't by wielding our authority or knowledge. Rather, when our own tenderness reaches out to connect with them through a childlike heart, a genuine relationship almost inevitably results.

Childlikeness is in the heart of every living person.

Childlikeness Will Grow

"Let our sons in their youth be as grown up plants, and our daughters as corner pillars fashioned as for a palace" (Psalm 144:12).

Here we see childlikeness joined with maturing roots that are deepened in the Lord. This applies to our own children, and to the child in us. Jesus emphasized this maturity when he sent out the 12. He said, "Be shrewd as serpents and innocent as doves" (Matthew 10:16).

This is childlikeness married with wisdom and stature. The stature will increase so that the child can carry weight in the spirit, but never by putting away the spirit of the child. The childlike heart grows up, held fast by the roots, the resolve, the strength, the understanding, and the wisdom to carry weight in the Spirit. This brings about the mature child of God.

Truly, the mature can be childlike, and the childlike can be mature. We all, no matter our age, have the same Holy Spirit inside of us. A four-year-old child can be rooted in their identity, secure, and with resolve in the Lord, entirely childlike. Simultaneously, older men and women can live powerfully, beautifully wise and learned and full of experience, yet still allowing themselves to be led by their own childlike spirit.

A CHILD WILL LEAD THEM

4

CHILDREN ARE FOR US

Changes of Mindset

We know that children access the same Holy Spirit that we do, and yet we tend to believe they are too little to meaningfully understand or contribute. But the more we walk with children, the more we become convinced that they are overflowing with spiritual understanding for us. *For* us.

Another old mindset is that children need to be taught what to think and taught to follow us. We want to tailor them to look like us. But the Father sees children differently, and the Bible offers us this evidence, that we should follow *them*. We can learn from them as much as they can learn from us—maybe even more. As we take on the Father's mindset, we humble ourselves in their presence so that we can become like them.

We go from seeing children as a distraction to recognizing them as a gateway. We try to eliminate distractions, but we open and enter through gateways. We find ourselves pleading with the Lord, "I want in. I am going to open that gate. Teach me. Remind me how to enter as a child."

Do you see how our mindset begins to shift?

It is popular culture to say that one day our children will change the world. But now we see that they are already fully capable of changing the world.

We used to think that teaching and training them ended when good behaviors were established. But now we see that true training of a child releases them into everything that the Lord has already said about them. We believe in them enough to call them up into who He has said that they are, and to position ourselves in faith, believing and hungry to receive of them this way. It releases all that Jesus is in them to come out of them.

We used to say things like "Shut them up; they're too loud," or the old adage, "Children should be seen and not heard." But now we long to hear what they have to say. We remember that in the temple, it was children who recognized Jesus when all the adults missed Him. We long to hear what they are shouting, singing, and talking about.

We used to think that kids who spend time in their imaginations are caught up in their little castaway world. But now we understand that they can see the atmosphere of Heaven. They can see angels. They can see Jesus standing right next to them.

Every day as we walk home from school, I ask my girls, "did you see Jesus today? Where was He?"

Inevitably, they see Him. "Yes, Mommy. I had a really hard time figuring out this problem and He helped me." They don't think of Him as distant, or believe themselves to be alone and dependent on their own strength. Their reality is that He is with them, helping them. They can actually see Him there.

We used to think, *They're just kids. Just wait until they get into the real world. There is no time for unicorns then.* But now we see their imaginations as the open doors for faith and the ability to see every heavenly thing. We learn to purposefully invite them into times of imagination. We encourage them to make up the craziest story they can think of. It seems so simple, but it is imperative we learn that their imagination can lead us and teach us. They believe with their whole hearts, and they can see what we can't see. They teach us faith.

Leah's Sons: For Her

Many of us are familiar with the story of Jacob, Leah, and Rachel. Jacob's heart was for Rachel, but Laban tricked him into first marrying her older sister Leah. Some versions of Scripture tell us that Leah was unloved; others go so far as to call her "hated." But in Genesis 29, we read that the Lord saw that Leah was unloved and that He opened her womb. Leah conceived and bore a son. And then comes the cool part. She birthed four boys, one right after the other. Her first son was named Reuben. Reuben means, "Behold, a son!" In Reuben, Leah literally discovered her identity. She realized who she was—a daughter of God. Here she was, in this adverse situation. She was insecure and jealous of her sister, trying to leech love from a reluctant husband. Yet the Father says, "I'm going to give you a baby, and then I'm going to give you another baby, and another baby, and another baby, and they're going to lead you in your process." And so, her first child was Rueben: Behold, I'm a daughter! I have a Father.

Leah gave birth to a second son, whom she named Simeon, which means, "Obedience." In Simeon, the Father was teaching Leah to listen to the Father, learn to obey His heart, and to hear Him and His precepts. He was opening her mind to the way that He thinks.

Then came Levi, which means, "A joining," or "to attach." Leah likely believed these boys would cause her husband to finally attach to her. But the Lord knew she had more process to go through. There was a joining and an attachment here, but it wasn't to her husband. Rather, it was a beautiful joining together of the revelation of her sonship. She's a daughter of the Father, becoming joined with the precepts of His nature. In everything she's learning in Him, she would become able to flesh out her sonship.

Do you see the prophetic process here? We all go through it. But who among us realized that our children could lead us into wholeness? As the Father brings them into our lives, He guides us intimately through our own becoming. As Leah welcomes each son, she learns her identity, learns the heart of her Father, learns to obey and trust Him, and learns to think like He thinks.

Leah's fourth son, Judah, marked a turning point for her. Up until his birth, she was still complaining and unfulfilled. She still wasn't as beautiful or as loved as Rachel, and likely never would be. And though none of her circumstances changed, with Judah came the ability to say, "I will praise the Lord." She was brought into her maturity as a daughter, fleshing out her sonship through the children that she birthed. In the same way, our children mark and guide our own personal processes of growth as we become whole in the Lord.

Our Children Open up What We See

There is a secret revealed in the story of Abraham, as father to Isaac, that is important for us to see and learn from.

Over the years, I have heard so many parents share vision and ideas—purposeful things from the heart of the Lord that are within them to accomplish. But these same parents often feel that when children come into the picture, all their passions must be put on hold, thinking those things must wait until our children get older.

Abraham did not see things that way. Abraham modeled a different perspective; he believed that the vision of the Lord he had seen *could only be accomplished* through his full, unreserved investment in Isaac. As a result, he engaged himself fully in Isaac's identity and destiny. Everything that Abraham envisioned would be opened up through his son.

As fathers and mothers, we not only call forth our children's identities, but we invest in and engage with their identities, training and walking with them in it. Seeing who they are actually gives life to what is in us to accomplish. We are in partnership with our children, and they are in partnership with us. The Father invested in Jesus so fully that they were one. Jesus said that if we see Him, we have seen the Father. All that the Father saw, this whole family of God all over the earth, could only come about through the identity of His Son. This is such a strong parallel to Abraham. His vision (which we are a part of!) came to pass through the identity of his son being walked out into reality.

So, I encourage you not to feel like your children are holding you back. Instead, see who they are and how who they are is actually opening up and giving life to your visions. Invest all that you are into them. This concept can open up the atmospheres of our homes. My children (and many children in my sphere) have begun to see people in their identity. They have even begun to call it out in me.

For instance, let's say we are in our car together, driving down the road. A young voice spontaneously offers itself from the backseat. "Mommy, do you know what's special about you?" It's important to recognize that moment. That is the Holy Spirit, pouring out of our kids, building up our families. Engage with them in this.

The Lord is faithful to open these things up in our homes as we believe what the Lord has said about our children, and as we call it to life. We carry them and we see the Spirit of the Father forming them.

Who children are in the Spirit becomes such a blessing to us. Because of them, we find ourselves experiencing the Lord, interceding, and being led into places of the Spirit because of who they are with us, for us…even leading us. We find that who Jesus is in them goes right into our core and ministers to us there, shaking that which needs to be shaken, and establishing us even deeper in Him.

Our children really do intercede for us. I have experienced one of my own children interceding for me. I was in worship one Sunday morning with our home church family but was not quite connecting. So, I knelt down and purposed in my heart to spend some time with the Lord. In that moment, my daughter Carabelle came over to me and sat on my kneeling legs. I was focused on my time with the Lord, but slowly my attention shifted, and I began to really hear what Carabelle was saying. She was groaning in the Lord. She was interceding for me. When I finally got to the place in the Lord where He wanted me to be, she got up and walked away.

As I encountered the Lord, my tears fell onto the carpet. But then I saw them seeping into the foundation of the church, literally becoming part of it. The Lord reaffirmed who I am, and my piece in the foundation of the church, the family He is building in the earth. Zeal stirred in me. We cannot quit! The promise is too big. We are a part of their foundation. Our love for them, and our love for the Lord, along with our belief in all that He is and has revealed to our spirits, are parts of their foundation. Yet, her presence and her intercession made a way for *me*. The spirit of children is for us in the same way that we say, "Our God is for us, not against us."

I would say that your children are for you as you are for them. Our children are interceding for us to see who we are, which in turn releases them to be who they are. We have to allow that process of the Lord in our lives.

As I learned more about the intercession of children, I was struck by the idea that Isaac went and reopened the wells that his father Abraham had dug. How did Isaac know where the wells were? He must have been with his father when they were dug and had a clear understanding of their value. He knew where the wells were, and he knew that they had to be reopened. He knew their value to the people. Likewise, I encourage you to trust that your children know the value of the wells you are digging right now in your life with Jesus. It may not always feel this way to you, but your children, in their spirit, know the value of those excavations.

Some parts of this vision have really stretched my life before the Lord. I have felt completely overwhelmed or simply *done,* not knowing what to do or where to go. In those moments, the Lord has gone into those places of my heart and called me up by allowing me to *hear* the intercession of children begging me not to give up or "sit this one out." They intercede for me to not throw in the towel. Their intercession reopens the wells within me that I had dug with the Lord years before.

I am telling you that the spirit of children all over the world is interceding for us to not give up or take a break. They pray for us not to quit when it gets hard, when the Lord is stretching us, or when He's pressing into us. The spirit of children all over the earth is interceding for us. Sometimes we want to step out of the game and just let the next generation figure this thing out. When I have reached these dark moments of complete exhaustion and frustration and pain in my process of becoming, weeping before Him, all I hear is their voices, the spirit of children interceding for us. Where there is struggle and stretching and pressing going on, your descendants and all the children, over 2,000,000,000 of them, all over the world, are interceding for you.

Esther

When it came time for Esther to go before the king, she was scared for her life. Most likely, she really didn't want to do what she needed to do. But her children, her people, interceded for her, and their intercession called her up to do what she needed to do. In turn, they were set free from the declaration of death upon their lives.

Esther was a queen, but she didn't really know how to walk as a queen who had the authority and purpose of the Lord in her steps. She didn't know how to walk it out. She was hidden and would have remained powerless by her own choice if she hadn't been called up by Mordecai and interceded for by her countrymen. The intercession of the children of Israel, the Jews, gave her the strength to press in and do what she had to do.

Can you hear them? The spirit of children is interceding for us to let the process and the work that the Lord is doing be completed.

I love how the Bible describes what happened at the end of that book of Esther. The adversity Esther faced was intense, and at the end of it all, after she has gone to the king and had essentially saved her people, we read,

Then Queen Esther, daughter of Abihail, with Mordecai the Jew, wrote with full authority... (Esther 9:29a)

How much authority? *Full* authority.

Esther did not have that authority right away. She had to endure a process that elevated her into the place where she knew she had full authority. She had to come up in her identity. The intercession of Mordecai, his family and the children of Israel was a big part of her pushing through her process. I don't think they were praying for her solely so that she could go before the king without receiving a death sentence. Their intercession carried her into full authority to do what needed done.

Do you see? This is so beautiful: she was for them, and they were for her. She did not have the strength without them. They had no freedom from the edict of death without her. Scripture reveals that by her command, Purim, the Jewish holiday to celebrate that redemption of the Jewish people, was established, and is still celebrated today.

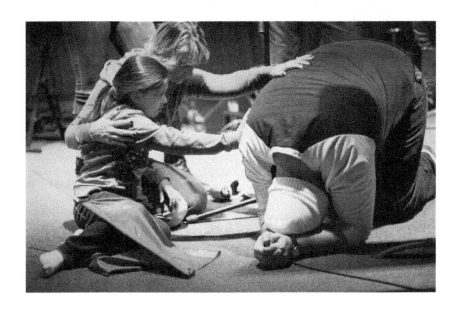

PART THREE

THE PARTNERSHIP

5

WALKING TOGETHER INTO THE PROMISE

As was our daily routine, I walked Rikka to her kindergarten classes one Wednesday afternoon. While there, I saw Amberle at recess. Though I knew she often spent that time playing with one or two other girls, today was different. She was on a swing and her usual friends were nowhere to be seen. I didn't recognize the little boy on the swing next to her. *Hmm.*

When she came home later that day, we began to talk. "How was school, Amberle?" I asked. She told me about her classes, her teacher, and her lunch… but didn't mention recess.

"I noticed that you were all by yourself at recess today. I didn't see any of the friends I usually see you with. I only saw a little boy on the swing next to you. Are you okay?"

Rikka chimed in at that point. "You looked lonely, Amber. I don't want you to be lonely."

Amberle immediately opened up and told us a most beautiful story.

"That boy is my friend Alec. He and I were talking about two things. We talked about *How to Train Your Dragon – Race to the Edge* because he *loves* dragons. And then we were talking about our friends, because we have friends being mean to us. We were saying that we still love them anyway."

I was surprised to hear Amber was experiencing mean friends and gently asked what had happened. She offered more insight, her sweet voice sharing itself without a hint of malice.

"Well, a little while ago, I was playing with all these girls. We were playing a game, and when I turned around to run, I didn't see that one of my friends was there behind me. I ran into her and fell on top of her. It was an accident. And all the girls knew that it was an accident, even the girl I fell on.

"But this other girl said I did it on purpose. And now she won't be my friend or let me play with them. Some of them come play with me at the beginning of recess, but I tell them that I know they love Grace too and that it is okay for them to go and play with her. They try to tell her it was an accident and ask her to let me be her friend again, but she still doesn't want to be my friend." Her voice trailed off gently as she finished her story. "But I still love her. She is still my friend."

Tears of joy welled in my eyes, my heart exploding with love and pride of who Amberle is. "Do you know how amazing you are? You love so well. You are such a good friend. Do you know you look so much like Jesus?"

"Oh yes, Mommy, I remember," she answered purely. "A long time ago, when I was like four or five, you read to me a story about Jesus and a guy's ear. And I remember how Jesus loved him."

Immediately, I knew she was referring to the story of the soldier who came to arrest Jesus in the garden. When Peter cut the soldier's ear off in defense of Jesus, Jesus put the ear back on the soldier and healed it—because He loved him.

I pulled Amber close. "You know there are people who don't know God. And there are some people who know about God and still don't want Him to be their friend. Sometimes people don't want to be friends with Jesus, even for 60 or 65 years. And yet Jesus still loves them. God loves all people, even the ones who don't love Him back. You are so much like Jesus, Amber. When I look at you, I see Him."

Her eyes were so bright and alive, they were almost dancing. "I look like Jesus, because Jesus has an open heart. And I have an open heart."

"Yes. Yes, you do Amberle," I said, weeping.

"And Mommy, you may think that when you read stories to me about Jesus that I don't seem interested. But my heart is listening. I love Jesus."

Tears streaming down my face, I took her in my arms and held her. "I know you do, Amberle. I know you do."

Usually with something like this, the momma bear inside me would rise up and forge ahead to make things right. But not this time. The momma bear in me couldn't even be found. I was so overtaken in her love, and her confidence in love. I could never even think to rob her of this experience. Her love and her Jesus were being deeply solidified in her spirit, at seven years old.

She is amazing. She shines like the brightest star, and she is not alone. Jesus has given us so many beautiful shining lights in our children. They are *His* children. He has so generously seeded them into our world. I am convinced, now more than ever, that these shining stars... yes, six, seven, and eight-year-olds...these children choosing to love and encouraging their friends on the playground to do the same...are already changing our schools and saturating our communities with hope, light, and love for all. They are not only doing the will of Him who sends us, but they are becoming the will of God on this earth by knowing who they are in Him and walking it out.

This is the food of Heaven among us, and Amberle offered us a very real example of it. Though she was cut off from a group of friends at school, there she was, sitting on the swings talking to a little boy, not only choosing the way of love for herself, but sharing with another how they could do this too. She was practicing being His love in the earth right now.

Our children are capable and hungry for the Jesus in us to walk with the Jesus in them. This is how the world changes: through hearts that are brand new and childlike, even when people hate You. We must love brand new. Let us do this and walk together with them, learning and becoming His will together.

PRAYER

We treasure these lights, Papa. We treasure their hearts. We treasure Your goodness inside them. Thank You for releasing them into our world. May we see You inside each one, in each and every child, even the ones who are broken and hurting and lashing out at such young ages.

May we love... just as Amber loves, just as Alec loves, just as You love. May we call to life the beautiful goodness and love that we know You have built within the DNA of every person. May we call them to life with our love. You are good, Papa...and perfect in all of Your ways. Thank You.

Training Young Children

I find that parents in the American church commonly believe that children ages 18 months up to about three years old should be in a nursery class instead of in worship with their family. Children this age are young and cannot express much, and often they have just learned how mobile they can be! It can be a challenge to hold onto them in the church setting. But I submit to you a different way. That time in their development is one of the most important times for them to be with you in worship gatherings. Much of a person's internal paradigm, including the way they will see God, the world, themselves, and how they will interact with others, is created in their very early years of life. These younger ones are in prime time for you to train and mold them. I know that concept might seem frustrating sometimes, but it is, in my opinion, one of the best times to have those children with us, learning and experiencing worship.

I was really intentional to train all of my daughters in worship when they were somewhere between two or three years old. I knew in the Spirit when it was time for each girl, and I literally got down on the floor with each one in the right moment, teaching them as I sat with them and sang over them. It was a process, but it was worth it.

I was singing in my kitchen one day, and Cara came up to me and sat in my lap. She raised my hand *for* me. No kidding. She came in and she put my hand where it was supposed to be as I was worshipping. She was, at such a young age, learning and connecting to a heart of worship to the Lord.

When that child is older, she will raise her own hands to Jesus in worship. Not because anyone told her to, but because it is in her heart to worship the Lord. I have never told my children they have to raise their hands to Jesus, but I did teach them worship, and they experienced my worship. From their youngest ages, experiencing my worship freed them to worship freely from their hearts too.

We must live this culture of worship and of Jesus with them *every day*. At home. At work. Everywhere we are. This is our culture. We give them the real Jesus and the real experience of Him in us.

This trains them. It shows them that they can connect with Jesus themselves, in their real every day.

One of my favorite passages on training children is in Deuteronomy 6, which details God's instructions about the Law. First, we need to understand that in the Old Testament, God gave those commandments to His people to teach them how to commune with Him. The Law was their way to His thoughts and heart. They didn't have the relationship with Him that we have through Jesus' covering of all our sin. They didn't experience that.

So, God gave them commandments to keep. Those requirements provided an opportunity for communion with Him.

> *These words, which I am commanding you today, shall be on your heart. You shall teach them diligently to your sons and shall talk of them when you sit in your house and when you walk by the way and when you lie down and when you rise up. You shall bind them as a sign on your hand and they shall be as frontals on your forehead. You shall write them on the doorposts of your house and on your gates* (Deuteronomy 6:6-9).

When we read this passage, we are reading about communion with the Father and the way to His heart. *Impress them on your children. Talk about them when you sit at home, when you walk along the road, when you lie down, when you get up.* If we read on in that passage, we even see counsel to tie them as symbols on your hands and bind them as signs on your forehead. Write them on the doorframes of your houses and on your gate!

The way you connect with Jesus in the presence of your children has to be your culture, meaning that it is consistent everywhere you are and everywhere you go. They have to see that the way to His heart is all over you. Give them the real Jesus.

Later in Deuteronomy, Moses forecasts a time when your sons will ask you, "Why do we do this? Why is this done in this way?" Moses' answer is: Tell them. Tell them from your real experience with Jesus. Tell them how you were slaves once and now you're free. Live openly with them. Give them the real Jesus. We do these things before our children while they're young.

Confirm Jesus in Your Children

In the middle of worship one morning, Rikka (who was four years old at the time) was playing with a little toy cell phone. I knelt down and told her that the only time mommy uses her cellphone in worship is to take a picture if I see Jesus somewhere.

I said, "Take my phone and look for Jesus. If you see Him, take a picture of Him!"

She clutched the phone in her fist, scanning the room. She was earnestly searching, looking at the faces of the people in that room. After a moment, she honed in on Denver, the worship leader. She walked right up and took three pictures of him, then came back to me. She saw Jesus so freely.

When children see Him, and when we start to see Jesus coming out of them, we confirm it. "Did you know that's Jesus you found? You found Him!" Isn't that what happened with Samuel and Eli? Samuel heard, but Eli confirmed. In the same way, we confirm that they are seeing and hearing the Lord, and that it is Jesus in them. Then we teach them and resource them. This is what we see with Andrew, who found the little boy with a lunch. Andrew saw what the boy had and took Him to Jesus. He resourced that boy's ability to offer food that would feed 5,000 people.

Agree with Your Child's Identity

As I wrote earlier, when our youngest daughter Cara was in my belly, the Lord told me she would be my Joseph. She would release in me the ability to dream and would increase my awareness of the activity of Heaven all around me. I took that to heart, and soon I recognized that my spiritual senses *were* increasing.

After she was born, I watched her closely and deliberately experienced her heart. I realized that she's a lover, much like, I imagine, the disciple John was, the "one that Jesus loved." That's Cara. She does not simply have a loving nature; her heart is literally on your heartbeat. She loves you in the deep heart places. I take time to practice with her, tuning to listen to each other's hearts. We talk about Jesus and practice hearing His heart. It becomes normal life. I walk with her in her identity.

Recently, I had a dream about her, in which a dear and highly-respected friend in our life came to me, pointed his finger at me, and declared, "Cara is a strong tower." I received that word over Cara without reservation. We are allowing it to open up in her; we walk together in it. "You're a strong tower Cara," I say. As she grows, these things will continue to unfold. As I remain believing, faithful, and willing, I will have opportunity to walk with her into those promises.

The Lord has taught me deeply through encounters with my own children. I clearly hear the voice of the Lord in them. For example, Rikka is expressive and creative, regularly making up songs and stories in her play. But as I listen, I hear portions of her songs or stories that are clearly the Lord. When those moments come, I encourage her, confirming her. "When you said that, Rikka, that was the Lord. When you did that, that was Jesus in you!" This is how she learns to recognize His voice, and His person revealed in her. She won't doubt it as she grows. Rather, she will live fully secure because she knows Him.

For some it can feel easier to receive from a child that they don't have to "deal with" at home every day. But let me encourage us that even in our own children, we can receive of Him. We can even receive the Lord in the children who bully our own.

Samuel: A Boy Given a Man's Message

When talking about these things with people, I find that many ask: *But how do we do this?* How do we facilitate an atmosphere where we actually see this? The kids that I'm with in my daily life, that I've adopted into my womb, how do I actually see this come out of them? There are no specific steps or processes, as we might wish, but there is a concept that will help establish the atmosphere we are looking for, and I see it when I look at Samuel and Eli.

The whole story of Samuel is crazy to me.

In 1 Samuel chapter 2, Samuel's mother, Hannah, took him to the tabernacle and gave him to the Lord, into the care of the priest, Eli. Samuel was raised there.

> *Now the boy Samuel was ministering to the LORD before Eli. And word from the LORD was rare in those days, visions were infrequent* (1 Samuel 3:1).

Now Samuel did not yet know the LORD, nor had the word of the LORD yet been revealed to him (1 Samuel 3:7).

We read that Samuel did not yet have a relationship with the Lord. Still, he heard the voice of the Lord and was entrusted with a weighty message, though he was only a boy. But we have to understand that bringing our firstborn son to Eli the priest was not like delivering him to the guardianship of one of our incredible pastors today, or even like giving him to someone who hears from the Lord all the time. If you were the mother and could submit your child to a pastor or a priest like that, you would feel confident that your kid would know the Lord.

But this was far from that. Scripture says that the word of the Lord was scarce in those days. Eli had not heard the Lord's voice in quite some time, and his sons were so rebellious that the Lord was angry with Eli. It was not a healthy church setting, and yet this woman came and trusted her son to the Lord in Eli.

And there Samuel was, a little boy only recently weaned from his mother. Then we read that Samuel heard the voice of the Lord... and didn't know who it was. So, Samuel ran to Eli, a first and then a second time, promptly responding in obedience to the only father he knew: Eli. "Here I am. You called me." And both times, Eli sent him back to bed, denying that he had called the boy. But when this occurred a third time, Eli discerned that the Lord was calling the boy, and his advice to Samuel changed.

And Eli said to Samuel, "Go lie down, and it shall be if He calls you, that you shall say, 'Speak, LORD, for Your servant is listening.'" So Samuel went and lay down in his place. Then the LORD came and stood and called as at other times, "Samuel! Samuel!" And Samuel said, "Speak, for Your servant is listening" (1 Samuel 3:9-10).

Not only did Samuel hear the voice of God, but *God came and stood by him.* This is not an impersonal encounter, nor is it the boy's imagination. This kid was experiencing the literal, tangible presence of God Himself standing right next to him in his room, talking to him.

In those moments, the Lord shared with Samuel a message so heavy and sobering that the Lord even said *both ears of everyone who hears it will tingle.* Samuel didn't experience a soft encounter with an "I love you" message, but instead received a foreboding prophecy for Eli.

To our thinking, this wasn't the message for a boy. Yet the Lord saw differently. This same capacity is in all kids, and if that's true, how much more should it be in our own children, who are in the culture of God's heart with us, hearing from Jesus every day?

God's message was a word of judgment concerning Eli's corrupt sons, who, because Eli refused to rebuke them, were going to be cut off with premature deaths. That is the message that the Lord endowed to that little boy! Would you tell your little kid that kind of message?

But the Lord entrusted it to a little boy. Furthermore, He *wanted* Eli to receive it through Samuel.

Jumping down to verse 15,

> *So Samuel lay down until morning. Then he opened the doors of the house of the Lord. But Samuel was afraid to tell the vision to Eli. Then Eli called Samuel and said, "Samuel, my son." And he said, "Here I am." He said, "What is the word that He spoke to you? Please do not hide it from me. May God do so to you, and more also, if you hide anything from me of all the words that He spoke to you"* (1 Samuel 3:15-17).

Do you hear Eli? He fully believes the Lord spoke to Samuel and he is hungry to hear it. This is how to create an atmosphere to hear and see the Lord in your kids. You get hungry. You must believe God's presence in them so fully that you get hungry. Hunger will translate through you in many different ways in many different scenarios. But if you are hungry, your full belief creates a hunger in you that will call forth what is in them.

It was not an option for Samuel not to share everything the Lord said with Eli, because Eli was craving the voice of the Lord. He had not heard that voice for a long time. He would do anything it took to get everything that the Lord gave to Samuel.

And that's our secret. I can't tell you specifically what that looks like in your home or classroom or neighborhood, but I can tell you that you have to get hungry to hear the Lord in your kids. Every time you're with kids, look for the Lord in them. Listen for Him. Search for everything the Lord has put in them. The spirit inside you, when you are truly hungry for what you are fully convinced is within them, will call that substance forth and release it to come out.

It is the same with adults. If you believe in me, if you have faith in me and want what is in me, then all that I have can rise up—and vice versa, when I believe in you. But if I don't believe in you, if I don't have faith in you such that I'm actually hungry for everything that's in you, even though you could have a whole wealth of treasure to give to me, I will receive nothing.

Hunger is what establishes the atmosphere.

Thus, Samuel grew and the LORD *was with him and let none of his words fail* (1 Samuel 3:19).

Not one word that Samuel uttered in the Lord fell void. The Father makes sure that everything that His children release in Him does not fail. He watches over them to perform His word in them.

6

ADVERSITY, RESISTANCE AND OVERCOMING

My family and I live less than a block from our neighborhood elementary school. About 900 children attend this school and hundreds of them walk by my house every day. A couple of years ago, one boy in particular routinely walked down the alley beside our home, saying ugly things. I began talking with Jesus about him, asking how I could get to his heart, to help him realize he could still be childlike and didn't have to be hard, angry, and mean. I knew his actual heart, though buried, was tender.

One day, when his words were uniquely awful and extreme, my heart burst forth and I said, "Sweetheart, you don't have to talk like that. Your heart is incredible. Your heart is so much better than that! You've got so much love in you!"

From that day in late October forward, everything changed. Happily, he no longer said those awful things anymore. For the rest of that year, when walking to school every morning, he literally did laps around the blocks around my house until I came out, so he could say hi to me. This boy was a sixth grader who was preparing to enter middle school, but the few sentences I offered him sank directly into his heart. He realized he still was allowed to be soft and tender. Inwardly, he craved that freedom so badly that he kept coming by, just to see my face and receive my smile. There are similar opportunities everywhere.

It's important that we understand that this heart and vision of the Father isn't only for kids who know Jesus or are growing up in believing families. It is for all children. I see kids in my spirit all over the world who see Jesus and hear His voice, but they don't know who it is they're experiencing. This is happening in Hindu and Muslim countries, in schools, in bedrooms, in kids on the street, and all over the world, even kids who are afraid, hurting, abused, and alone. They are all seeing and hearing Him, and all they need is for a mama or papa to rise up and say, "That's Jesus! That's Jesus talking to you! When you hear that voice, it's Him! He is with you. He has always been with you." The more you confirm it, the more quickly they will recognize His presence, and His voice talking to them.

This understanding is what motivates everything in our work with them, in every place we relate with children. They are a part of us. They are hearing Him. We must not go forward without them.

To Walk with Rikka, in Her Identity

For a period of several months, Rikka began to experience a hard, divine period of resistance. Everywhere we went, she received a remarkable amount of mocking and correction. She seemed to encounter rejection and adversity from every angle, from both adults and children, strangers and friends. This increased all at once. It was hard, and I was unnerved in my spirit. I remember asking the Lord what in the world was going on. "God, I don't understand what is wrong with my child right now. She is perfect and beautiful. Why such adversity?"

One day, when we were walking to pick Amberle up from school, Rikka skipped alongside me as we cut down a back alley, singing a song she had made up. To this day, the lyrics are engrained in my spirit: *God is here. I need you to see Him. I need you to see Him. You don't have to be afraid. He is here.*

If I could have stopped time and had a kumbaya moment in the middle of that alley, I would have. As it was, I had to be on time to meet Amberle's dismissal bell. But that song was the Lord. The Spirit of the Lord was coming out of Rikka and releasing a holy call through the streets of our town. I was overtaken in it. As we arrived at the kindergarten playground, 20 or 30 parents were standing there, waiting for their children. Rikka's skipping continued (in her mind at that moment, she was a beautiful unicorn).

Suddenly, Rikka boldly began telling everyone the story of Shadrach, Meshach, and Abednego, all the while still galloping on her pretend horse on that public school playground. She told everybody about these guys that got thrown into the furnace. As she trotted to the middle of the playground, she turned around and shouted, "And God came to them! He came to them in the fire!"

Every parent was brought to complete silence, staring at my little daughter in the center of the playground. She captured and transformed the atmosphere on that playground. I stood there with no idea what to do. My brain was acutely aware of how many people were around us, but I knew I had to let her go. Jesus was obviously doing something in her, and I didn't want to interrupt it.

One parent caught my eye. The Spirit of the Lord was all over her, such that she could not speak. As we gathered up Amberle and turned to go home, this mother came over to me. Her eyes bored holes into mine. "How does that little girl know that about me?"

The Spirit of the Lord was pursuing people by the prophetic words pouring through my four-year-old daughter that day, leaving them unable to speak. Every kid has this same Jesus, this same Spirit, on the inside, ready to be released. Each will look and sound different, as they all have different personalities and gifts and callings. But it is *Him*, and He will call to all of us.

When we got home, I sent the girls off to play, knowing I needed time to process what I had just experienced. Immediately the Lord put it all together within my spirit. His voice was very clear. "Jocelyn, Rikka must experience adversity to walk out her call."

We as adults slowly come to terms with the purpose of adversity in our life; we begrudgingly acknowledge that the process is *for* us. We have seen that adversity calls us up. Children need the same opportunity and process, even at four years old. We have to understand that. What's more, we must walk with them in it. We can't shield them, correcting everyone who brings them adversity. We walk with them, confirming Jesus in who they are and calling them up. We remind them that whether people love them or hate them, they have the word of the Lord inside them, and that we will stand with them. We teach them how to keep their hearts soft and open to people, while remaining strong and full of boldness to declare the thoughts of God... because this is who they are.

The vision of the Father for children is not easy. We look at it from afar and see that it will change the world, and it feels so encouraging. But when it comes down to the everyday, and it's our kid who's being picked on, the glamorous, picturesque hope takes on a profound weight. It is the Lord, in those moments! In them is our opportunity to walk with our children. This is how His heart for these children will unfold, as our feet walk right next to theirs. We see everything that happens through their identities. We see it through the Father's eyes, and what He sees in the spirit of our child. Then we can walk with them in it. Time and time again, we train, empower, reaffirm, and confirm for them who Jesus is in them, who they are in Him, and how that walks through everyday life.

In this way, we find the Lord, diligently seeing Him in all things. All things. We don't just see Him in the easy-to-find-Him times, but also in these real life, rubber-meets-the-road situations. We have to see Him in everything. Every piece is spiritual. Every step with our children is in the Spirit.

So even in the difficult times, when there are things that you do not necessarily associate with this vision of the Father for children, in the things that are easily labeled as natural results or worldly obligations, we now see the Father. We see all things through His eyes and through the identities of our children.

If our children are learning this at four or five years old, and they are already changing atmospheres, already releasing things that are calling people in our towns to the Lord, just imagine what it will look like as they continue to grow stronger in their influence in the earth. They are changing the world!

PRAYER

Thank you, Father. Thank you for children. Thank you for Your heart for children. We are just so honored that we get to walk with these little feet. What a beautiful gift You have bestowed on us in our children. We don't take it lightly.

We receive them, every one of them. May we see them all around us and receive all of them into our womb.

We stand with them.

Father, You are life. Your very presence is released among us through children. Awaken us, Father. Awaken the spirit of a child in us as we are with them. Amen.

Children Who Seem Spiritually Asleep

Let's spend a few minutes encouraging those who feel frustrated. They can see that all of this is in their child, but their child seems spiritually asleep. When we become fully convinced of what we see in the Father's heart for kids, we start to see all that is within our children. We see so much, but there are times when the children seem asleep. They are not truly connecting to what is within them. They seem disengaged.

Have you ever felt that way?

Call to mind the story in Acts 20, when Paul was preaching late into the night. Midnight came and went, and on Paul spoke, responding to the hunger of the people. We read in Scripture that there was a boy named Eutychus sitting in a window on the third floor. Eventually, he drifted off to sleep, fell out of the window, and died on the street below.

He was not engaged.

Paul walked over, laid on the boy, and said, "There is life in this one." And the boy came alive.

When you feel like your child is disengaged, or even sleeping in their spirit, there is yet life in them. Resist the impulses to nag at them or to become angry and frustrated. Sometimes we over-correct, doing all we can think of in our human efforts to make them stay awake. Instead, consider what it might look like to go to the exact place where they are, and be *with them there*. Go, in the gentle and confident strength of love, and speak life. The Lord meets us right where we are, and He does this with our children, too. He is with our children.

In fact, let's consider this further. Young Eutychus ultimately experienced a tremendous thing! Because he was allowed to be as he was and was met by Paul there (who simply yet purposefully went and laid down right there with him, not in alarm but in the power of the Holy Spirit), he got to experience dying and coming back to life! Eutychus experienced being raised from the dead!

We cannot force our children, especially as they get older. We love them, we believe in the identity given to them, and we call it out in them. But if they walk through a season of sleepiness, the Lord can show Himself to them even there. Put your trust in the goodness of the Lord, their Father. Meet with Him in prayer. This may be the season in which they will see something so big come upon them from the Lord that it will change their life.

So, be encouraged.

Sometimes, it can seem to us that a child doesn't want to interact with us. When we sense this, it is critical to take on God's viewpoint. We know that each child is created in the image of God, who has already received us. Jesus' own words in Mark show us that Jesus is in them to the point that when we receive them, we receive Him. Accordingly, when we feel like a child doesn't want to embrace us, we remind ourselves of what is true: *Jesus is in this child, and I know Jesus wants me.* Therefore, we become convinced of Heaven's reality: *deep in their hearts, this child wants to receive me.*

Do you see how this changes the way we work with children? We pour out confidently, assured that they want to receive from us. If a child initially pushes you away, the way to connect with them is through your ability to be childlike. This is a heart-to-heart language that all children speak. It is a love that is affectionate, unoffendable, and easily believes.

Childlikeness in us says "I believe in you. I don't care what you did yesterday. I believe in you." That is how you get to their heart.

Gideon and Jether

You may remember the story in Judges 7, when God whittled the Israelite army from 10,000 down to a mere 300 men. Gideon and these men fought the resulting battle against the Midianites with torches and pitchers. Soon their enemy was fleeing their camp, with Israel in hot pursuit. Gideon knew that he needed to go after them and finish what the Lord laid before him to accomplish. He refused to leave his mission half-done. The enemy was to be completely annihilated. As the story continues, two kings were captured and brought to Succoth, and 70 doomed leaders from that city were brought out to their deaths. Then, Gideon addressed his firstborn son, Jether.

So he said to Jether his firstborn, "Rise, kill them." But the youth did not draw his sword, for he was afraid, because he was still a youth (Judges 8:20).

We see that Jether was just a scared young boy; he couldn't bring himself to carry out the task his father Gideon laid upon him. I asked the Lord why Gideon took his young son with him in the middle of this battle, and why he wanted him to make the kill. When I looked up the meaning of Jether, I received my answer. Jether means, "one that excels, abundant, excellent." Suddenly, I could see Jether's identity, and I realized why Gideon had done what he did. Because of who Jether was, Gideon had to take his son with him and show him what it meant to leave nothing undone.

Excellence requires this. If we're doing it, we're doing it all. It will be done with quality and to completion. They could not allow the enemy to escape. They needed to finish the job entirely. Gideon needed to walk this out with his boy, because this was the boy's identity. He was training him. He did not scold the boy for not being able to make the final blow; in some ways, don't you think Gideon might have anticipated that?

But all the more, Gideon stepped up to train Jether in his identity, and he showed the boy how to be who he was called to be. Ultimately, Gideon dealt the final death blows himself, but he chose to have his son there and engaged with what he was doing, to train him in who he was.

And so, we understand why the boy was taken to the battlefield with his father. The child whose identity was named "Excellence" was being shown what excellence, in its fullest and boldest sense, looks like.

Do you see how it all comes together? In walking with them in everyday life, His heart unfolds. And it will change the world. So, talk with your children. Be very real. It's not complicated. Jesus is simple.

7

LIVING WITH CONVICTION

One afternoon several years ago, it was nearly time for my children to take their afternoon naps. As a wise mother does, I invited Rikka to jump with me on the trampoline in the hopes of tiring her out for a long nap. While we were jumping, I looked up and saw a weighty cloudiness in the sky. A red car passed by our home and I saw an evil spirit influencing the driver. My heart ached and I began to pray.

Then I began to sing, "Lift up your heads. Lift up your heads. Jesus, Yours is the Kingdom. Yours is the power. Yours is the glory forever." Over and over again I sang this. I sang it over our neighbors, over the school close to us, over the parents of every student. Over and over. And there we were, still jumping. I thought of a song Rikka had created recently and often sang around the house. I asked her if she remembered it. Immediately she began singing it again: "Just believe. Believe in your heart. Like a unicorn that flies into your heart. Believe. Jesus is in your heart. Believe. Just believe!" I joined her. I told her that Jesus gave her that song and that she needed to sing it, to give it to all the people around us. She sang it again and again as we jumped.

Completely winded from jumping and singing at the same time, I suggested we go back inside. But as we walked from the backyard into our kitchen, I felt no release to be done in the Spirit yet. I sensed that I needed to press in because there was much more awaiting. There was an assignment, a purpose, and some travel in the Spirit would be necessary to take me there.

By instinct, I checked social media and was drawn into an urgent pleading for prayer for those being violently attacked by a terrorist organization. I combined the songs Rikka and I had been singing; they became intercession that poured out of me. I felt an urgency to sing it over and over. Rikka heard me and joined me in the kitchen. I told her about this group of people who don't know Jesus loves them and they don't know that they are His, and so they hurt people and are very mean to little kids. I asked her to sing her song for them. Immediately, she began to sing and pray, with her hands clutching her heart, for these people to believe that Jesus is in their hearts. "You don't have to be mean. You don't have to be afraid. Just believe that Jesus is in your heart."

I was so overtaken in the Spirit of Jesus as He drew me in through Rikka's prayer and song. I sang my song and she sang hers, both at the same time. After a few minutes, Rikka seemed to feel release, so she got up and went to play. But I was still drawn into the Spirit even more now than before; Rikka had opened something up in me that I could not leave. It was nap time, so I put Rikka and Cara down for their naps, and went back down to the kitchen to continue pressing in.

In the following moments, I was taken in the Spirit over some mountain tops into a village. And I began to sing over the children, over the families, over the hard, terrorizing hearts that I met. I literally traveled the world that day. I saw my heart joined to people that I have never met in my natural body, but I know them and their faces in my spirit. "Lift up your heads. Believe. Only believe in Jesus. His is the kingdom, His is the power, His is the glory forever." Over and over again, my lips sang as my spirit released, "Jesus, Yours is the kingdom, Yours is the power, Yours is the glory forever!"

I began to pray and intercede. Soon I saw weapons falling to the ground. As I walked through this place, from a kingdom of love, in the nature of Jesus, I saw men falling to their knees. Some men fell backwards, backs flat to the ground, as their hearts surrendered to His Presence there with them.

Then, in a few seconds, I saw all of them in my womb… and I wept. I saw children, parents, and even their attackers; all of them were in my womb, and I began to sing over them. "Peace, be still. Come all who are weary, rest in me. Love has overtaken your minds. Now may Jesus cause your spirits and hearts to come alive."

As a mother does, I began stroking their hair and singing a lullaby over them, reassuring them that their Daddy was not mad at them, but loved them. "Peace, be still. Trust me. Rest in me." I was their mother, and they were my children, every one of them. The lullaby lulled their minds to sleep and gave their spirits freedom to connect with the Lord. Before long, there came a moment of release. As I continued singing my lullaby over them, I whispered, "Daddy. It's time."

The Father got up and walked into their midst. I continued to sit there, rocking back and forth, singing my lullaby as He came in. There was rest. Peace. Trust. Hearts were ready to meet with Him. Resting in this place, the lullaby continued ever so softly, until it faded in the stillness of hearts resting in this beautiful Present One.

Later, after I was able to get up and resume my everyday tasks, I became curious about Rikka's song. What did the unicorn mean? I had disregarded that part earlier when I was caught up in the Spirit, but now I wanted to know. I don't ever want to miss anything. So, I looked it up. *What does unicorn mean?* I found that unicorns symbolize a spirit of purity, innocence, and childhood. They are single-minded, walking a straight path. In the old days, it was a team of horses pulling a carriage.

Rikka's song pleaded for us to believe, just like a unicorn flies into your heart, through imagination, through faith in the Person Jesus. Her heart was the gateway for everything I experienced in the Spirit that day. And in Him, in our belief that He is, we can be single-minded, a family joining together as one, wholly following after the Lord, taking a direct path to His heart. Through our childlike belief and imagination, we can feel and see all that He holds in His heart. We join together with our children to intercede for weighty things.

In 2 Chronicles 20, we read that Israel and Judah experienced several years of peace. But then, all of a sudden, three armies joined together against Israel. The people came to King Jehoshaphat in terror, crying, "We're surrounded!" King Jehoshaphat was afraid. Scripture is very specific on how he called the people together: "I need you, your wives, your infants, and your children." No one was to be left out as the nation assembled to address this threat.

All Judah was standing before the LORD, with their infants, their wives and their children (2 Chronicles 20:13).

As a mother, I have very different inclinations. The last thing I want is for my kids to be afraid. If I am going to a meeting to discuss avoiding the annihilation of our entire nation by an enemy army that is on the hilltop waiting to attack, I would want to shelter my children from becoming aware of this terror. Wouldn't you do the same thing? But that is not what happened. Their children were a part of them in seeking the Lord. This is a beautiful picture of seamless community, together as one. Whenever we are tempted to believe that our children aren't ready for the weighty or terrifying things, we must renew our minds to understand that they are a part of us. We need them as part of the whole, together with us.

The nation of Israel and Judah sought after the Lord together. People of all ages. King Jehoshaphat said to the Lord, "This is our land. This is our place of inheritance to live and to worship. This is where Your name is, in Your house. And these people are going to take us out. But we are seeking You and our eyes are on You."

Can you feel the power of that oneness?

And the Lord responded. Quickly, His Spirit came upon one of the men and he began to speak the word of the Lord. It's a beautiful picture of what happens when we are together in the fullness of the Lord, in a seamless community where our children are actually part of us, not set apart and sheltered.

Instead, we draw them in to their rightful places among us.

Seeing Differently

Once we see and hear the call and invitation of the Lord, the promise of God changes us. We do not ever see the same way again. It is the same when we see the heart of the Father in our children. When we see the promise in them, when we see the promise in each other, we will never see the same way again.

> Now when Abram was ninety-nine years old, the Lord appeared to Abram and said to him, "I am God Almighty; Walk before Me, and be blameless. I will establish My covenant between Me and you, And I will multiply you exceedingly." Abram fell on his face, and God talked with him, saying, "As for Me, behold, My covenant is with you, And you will be the father of a multitude of nations" (Genesis 17:1-4).

The verses that follow detail the covenant of God and the inheritance of Abraham. Rest assured, from the time God first promised Abraham that his descendants would outnumber the sand on the shore and the stars in the sky, Abraham never saw life the same way again. And though Sarah was likely a beautiful woman, he never saw her the same way again, either. She was no longer merely his pretty wife. Now he saw the promise she would carry. He saw the promise in everything. When he walked about the land, he saw that his children would outnumber the dust. He saw them outnumbering the stars. Everywhere he looked, in his wife, in his children, in the land, and everywhere he went, he saw the promise. It changed him, and everything he did came through the filter of that promise.

Likewise, in everything we do, especially as we're raising our children, and as we interact with the many children we encounter on a daily basis, everything is different because of the promise He revealed to us. He bestows this promise on us, calling us to be mothers and fathers. We begin to actually see children the way He sees them. We start to walk the land, realizing the weight of the promise upon us all. We cannot help but to carry it and carry them, faithfully and in full belief. Our interactions with them change. Everything about us begins to align with how the Father sees them and engages with them.

How the Father trusts children! We realize that every step of our lives with them is important and is sowing seeds into the earth of this promise. It will come forth! We cannot idly sit by and forget about it. We cannot allow ourselves to lose focus with them. Who they are, who Jesus is in them, and the promise of Father's heart towards them; all of these are important.

Walking with Greater Conviction

In Deuteronomy, we see the promise of love to a thousand generations of those who love God and keep His commands. He is faithful to every promise He has spoken, unto a thousand generations! I would urge us not to sit out, hoping that the next generation to come down the line will capture the vision of the Lord we see for children. That will cost the children of our generation their destiny. Let us live with the conviction that our lives matter, and as a result, our children will walk into this promise right now, with us.

Call to mind how the Israelites spent 40 years wandering in the desert. The journey from Egypt to Canaan, the Promised Land, should have taken only days. But because of their grumbling, unbelief, and disobedience, a whole generation had to die off, and a whole other generation be born, for the faith to arise for them to enter in. God forbid that we lose focus, at the cost of a whole generation. We and our children can be the ones to walk into this promise. It is our privilege to walk into this with them. Our own childlikeness can see the promise of the Lord for the world in the childlike spirit, if only we walk with intentional, joyful conviction of its weight and reality. There is divine purpose in every step we take with our children. We don't have to make rounds in the desert like the Israelites did. But we can if we choose to, if we don't realize the weight of this promise and receive it in the faith that changes the way we walk.

So, walk uprightly! Walk in love with your Father, in full belief of His promise, sight, and heart for your children. Walk with them. It's not okay to throw in the towel when all this starts to feel overwhelming and hard. We cannot quit. We must choose to engage with our children and with the One who created them and placed this promise inside of them, at all times, not just when our kids make us proud and fill our hearts. Yes, then, but also when it is hard, and when we feel exhausted and frustrated. *Especially* then.

By faith, we must engage with them, just as we engage with each other. We engage with them and with the Lord in them. In simple ways, engage with them. Share what's on your heart. Open yourself and ask what is on their hearts. If they have a tendency towards specific arenas, be with them there. Walk with them in the promise in their everyday life and personality.

My daughter Rikka loves to make up her own songs; she's very prophetic. While we were sitting on the back porch of our home one afternoon, I asked her to imagine with me that we were walking down an alleyway and through a specific part of our town. We looked into the houses to see the people, and I asked her to tell me what song she heard the Lord singing to those people.

She began to sing, "Jesus is alive. He's right here. He's in you."

It can be that simple.

In those moments, because I live in the conviction of who she is, I engage with the identity and the promise of the Lord in my child. As we continue to walk together and engage in His heart for children which is alive in her, it will be opened up more and more.

We need to purposefully engage our children in everything we do in life. This allows us to not only engage with them, but also allows them to walk with us. They can observe the real living Jesus in us. They see our relationship with the Father. They see us repent. They see us choose to believe. They see us worship and pour out our hearts. They see us forgive. They see us study Scripture. And in all of these things, they engage with us as we engage with them.

When the prophet Ezra was repenting, Scripture says that all these people began to gather around him: men, women and children. Ezra let every one of them in. He lived wide open to them, and they could experience his repentance with him.

The book of Ezra also clarifies to us that when the Law was read, anyone who was able to understand the words was to be present. If the person was old enough to understand what was being spoken, they were supposed to listen with the adults.

In the same way, we let children walk with us and see all of our lives. Kids are a part of us in all things.

Though I'm more regularly with the elementary kids on Sunday mornings, I recently spent a morning in the preschool room, helping out. It's always really fun to spend time with three- and four-year-olds. We talked about Jesus being the Good Shepherd, but we had extra time after our lesson, so we were having snacks and playing. Some were building with blocks, and a few of us began to play pretend.

Little Erica began to tell us she was our teacher. It was hilarious to watch her command the room, teaching and sternly correcting us as her pupils. I began to sing in her classroom, just to rile her up. We were having a fun game, laughing hysterically. After a few minutes, she picked up the dry eraser and pretended it was a cell phone, sternly saying to me, "I'm going to have to call your father!" She appointed three-year-old Thijs as my father, who immediately assumed his role. He walked over to where I was sitting on the floor, put his hand on my shoulder, and said, "Hey, honey. I'm your father. Boo!" It was hilarious. But ever since that moment, my spirit felt the weight of young Thijs's words, *I am your father.*

I tell you, that child knows how to be a father. He is young but he has the anointing of a father on him. Almost every day of every week since then, I've said to the Lord, "I will let You father me through him." Something so tangible came on me. I felt a three-year-old father in him, caring for me.

God has no age. Holy Spirit has no age. He can care for us. He can lead us. He can open us up. He can do as He will, through any age, old and young, even a baby.

I want to receive from them. All of us can. It's in our awareness. When you believe something, you have access to it. It's important that we fully wrap ourselves around what the Lord has shown us is in our children, believing it for all it's worth. It is our faith and belief that enable us to access His promise.

Think about Rebekah. Maybe she didn't handle the situation perfectly, but Rebekah loved her son Jacob and believed his identity so much that she was willing to do anything, walk anywhere, and walk through anything with him, to see it come to pass (see Genesis 25-27). May that kind of tenacity be stirred up in us, to fight for and walk with our children with that kind of conviction and devotion.

We also see this in Deborah's time as a judge over Israel.

Until I, Deborah, arose, Until I arose, a mother in Israel. (Judges 5:7b)

Scripture details that a time came when Deborah's heart shifted, taking up the posture of a mother of her nation in her heart. A similar shift must happen in us, in which our hearts are convicted about our children. With the heart of mothering comes strength and real authority.

Later in the same book of Judges, we read about Jael, the woman who drove the tent peg through the enemy general's head as he slept. The general had come to that house because he believed those who lived there to be a safe ally.

Woven together, these two stories show me a specific encouragement concerning our children, who trust us and lay their thoughts down before us. There are times as mothers when we discern that specific thoughts are plaguing our child. In those places of thought, where our children lay the troubles in their minds in our hands, we have the authority to drive those things out. The Lord will show you how. You will work through those things with your children, showing them where their thoughts have departed from the character of Jesus, coaching them which thoughts to let go of. You can walk them through that process. There is a real place for you in the conviction of the Lord to arise as a mother in strength, and take these poisoned things out of your children's lives.

We see a weighty demand for conviction in Jesus' words in Matthew 18:

> *But whoever causes one of these little ones who believe in Me to stumble, it would be better for him to have a heavy millstone hung around his neck, and to be drowned in the depth of the sea* (Matthew 18:6).

This is such a heavy, passionate statement. We can plainly see that Jesus *really* cares about kids. We don't often hear Him speak that strongly. His words here reveal that He carries our children. He loves and believes in them, and passionately wants us to receive them. We must become so convicted of who they are and that He is within them that it impacts the way we walk with children.

The Conviction to Multiply the Seed

There are many Scriptures where we see the Lord talking to parents about the kids that would come through them. He gave them pictures of what they would be like. For instance, He told Zacharias, "It is he who will go as a forerunner before Him in the spirit and power of Elijah, to turn the hearts of the fathers back to the children..." (Luke 1:17a). These words are way bigger than one child. He was seeing the seed of Abraham. He was seeing the promise of God over generations that came from one seed. The seed multiplies and grows.

I encourage you, as you father and mother your children, multiply your seed as in the parable of the talents. Intentionally think of it that way. Remember when the servant had been given five talents and made five more? What did the Lord do? He multiplied it even more. So, as you're raising your children, get a renewed picture of who your children are, and then multiply the seed in everything, and in every opportunity.

When I think about multiplying the seed, I picture a seed in my hand. That seed can be something the Lord has told me about my child, something I see in my child that looks like the Lord, a prophetic word spoken over my child, or a promise of the Lord I have found in Scripture for children. Whatever the seed is, I look for ways to grow it and multiply it. By faith I pray it over them. I talk about it with them. When I see opportunity, I walk into it with them, reminding them of that seed. Those seeds are always at the front of my heart and mind as I walk with them. This is how we multiply the seed. We posture ourselves in full faith, and we step into it the best we know how. We believe, we practice, we pray, and we let the Lord open it up.

Let Us Walk This Thing out Together

When I am with the Lord, I see a table. It is the Lord's table, piled high with the best food of Heaven. The best pieces of Himself are prepared for us and served here. This table is prepared for children, alongside us. For a short period of time, children can only drink milk. Then they are introduced to food. In the story of Abraham and Isaac, when Isaac was weaned, Abraham threw him a feast. When the time had come for Isaac to drink only milk no longer, it was as though Abraham was declaring, "Look what you get to eat for the rest of your life!"

Milk in this analogy equates to our knowing. I know Jesus loves me. It's really good. We talk about it and meditate on it. We love its goodness in our whole self. But the meat of it, or the food and substance for our being in His image, comes when we walk it out. Food is when we live and do the things of our Father, when we walk out what it looks like to be loved and to *become* love. We can feast around this table, walking this thing out together with our children. Jesus said that His food was to do the will of Him who sent Him.

In thinking about this, what do you see? This is the table where we get to feast with our children. We get to not just talk about God's love; we get to live it out. That is the feast, and we get to feast at this table with our children. Not only are we made brand new (childlike) every day, and not only can we connect and bring forth the child in everyone around us, but we now see also that we get to feast around the table and walk it out together with them. We get to learn how to become His living desire in the earth, with our children. We are all children of God, and we are all learning. They are children, and they are learning. We can do this together.

The prophecy about the coming Messiah we saw in Isaiah said *a child will lead them*. Later, in Matthew, we read, *"Behold the Virgin shall be with child and shall bear a son, and they shall call His name Immanuel,' which translated means, 'God with us'"* (Matthew 1:23).

Jesus did not just become "God with us at" 30 years of age. He was Immanuel as a baby, as a child. God is with you in a child. A child will lead them *as a child*, not when they grow up and start thinking straight. Don't change their thinking. Jesus was 12 years old when He sat in the temple conversing with the scribes and the teachers, the know-it-alls of that time. He was able to fully converse with them, and they were in wonder at Him.

When is the last time we did that in church? I am personally in heaven when we all come together in our church gathering times and sit in a circle and find ourselves in wonder at the wisdom coming out of our kids, at the secrets of the Kingdom that are coming out of our kids. I rejoice when we marvel at their dancing that established an atmosphere in the middle of the room, because of kids being kids. That is Heaven to me.

> *"And it shall be in the last days,"* God says, *"That I will pour forth of My Spirit on all mankind; And your sons and your daughters shall prophesy, And your young men shall see visions, And your old men shall dream dreams"...* (Acts 2:17)

All of us, young and old, can experience prophetic dreams and visions. It's important to carry your children's dreams with sobriety. Ask your kids what they're dreaming about.

Because of these things, I am personally passionate that our kids not be sequestered away from us in a classroom for our entire meeting every Sunday. I know a lot of churches have entirely separate programs for children while they're on the premises, and I am not criticizing those ministries. But I will tell you my experience of how that affects children long-term. I have observed that children age out of children's programs at 11 years old with no understanding of how they fit in the church, or in their local congregation. In the years between their birth and middle school, we as the church body have missed out on all the prepared praise, prophecy, and other beautiful things that the Lord laid within them.

Many times, they transition into youth programs without any critical possession of how welcome, accurate, and necessary their presence is to the entire church. Of course, our children and youth benefit from set-apart times to connect, build relationships among their peers, and learn together; I simply wish our children were intentionally drawn into the full church congregation more often, and with greater hunger.

Such times together can train us in appreciation of one another and in partnership together. If children come in and don't know their place of belonging in the family, or don't feel confident in their value and purpose among us, we should endeavor to adjust quickly. We want them to know they are an integral part of who we are, and that our understanding of the Lord is incomplete without them.

There are a few ways we do this as a church family. Our children are a part of our praise and worship almost every time we gather, and they join the full adult gathering every four weeks or so, even for the sermon. When we are in times of ministry, we bring children right into it with us. If someone goes to pray for another, they take a child with them to be a part. We purposely include them. We also look for things that they have shared or written about and invite them to share it with the whole family. Their simple words, impressions from the Spirit, and purity in prayer is life, healing, and encouragement to the body. This is the way we posture our hearts towards them. It can take shape in many ways, but I encourage you to intentionally find ways to draw children in and receive from their spirit whenever you gather.

8

MOTHERING AND FATHERING OUR CHILDREN

Every day as I walk my daughters to school, I tell them who they are. I boldly reinforce their unique identities.

When Amber was in second grade, I would say, "Amber, you're my bright and shining star. Your kindness. The way you love and befriend all people is such grace from God. You really are the brightest creature on the planet. You are a shining star. Such beautiful, brilliant light." I told her this every day.

Then I would ask, "How are you going to be light to your classmates today? What are you going give from your heart to your teacher today? What do you want for your school today? You get to walk through the hallways and pray those things into the school!"

That year she made a new friend, and soon it began to seem that this little girl, who we will call Mercy, was Amber's one and only friend. Because I was not at school with her every day and couldn't see if it was a healthy friendship or not, I reminded Amber frequently that she could have more than one friend. But she just kept talking about Mercy, and only Mercy, all the same.

A few weeks later in the evening after school, there came a surprise knock on our front door. I opened it to see a young man in his mid-twenties, who introduced himself as Mercy's uncle. He said that Mercy was insisting on a play date with Amberle, and wondered if she, and two other little friends, could come into our home to play. We welcomed this spontaneous party of little girls, who skipped outside to play together in our backyard.

A beautiful picture of evangelism took shape in our home. The kids were playing and picking flowers. My husband was changing the spark plugs on our vehicle; the uncle rolled up his sleeves and joined in to help. We built a quick rapport and enjoyed this spontaneous time together. It was perfect. As it got dark, we all came in the house and the kids went upstairs to continue their play.

Chris and I sat down in our kitchen with the uncle, continuing our chat. He began openly sharing his story with us. Growing up out West, he had been homeless as a teenager. I took the opportunity to ask about Amber's friend Mercy. "Tell me about her family. Is there any way I could meet her mom and connect with her?" I couldn't help but notice the uncle's face shift uneasily. He hesitated, his body language revealing tension. I could tell I had walked into uncomfortable territory.

Finally, he began to tell us about the dynamics of Mercy's home. I can't even begin to describe how complicated it was. It is still to this day one of the messiest situations I have ever encountered. The thought that a child was growing up in the middle of this kind of thing was so grievous to my spirit. Chris and I purposefully sat there calm and open, to help the uncle feel comfortable and safe.

But inside, I was grieving and interceding for Mercy and for all the relationships that were happening in the home. The family unit was chaotic and complicated. Then I felt the mama bear in me rising up. I began panicking internally, wrapped in fear for my daughter. "Oh no," I thought. "What am I going to do? How am I going to protect Amber from experiencing this mess?"

After several hours of play, the uncle left with our three new friends. We sent the girls upstairs to brush their teeth while I freaked out to Chris on the couch. I was fearful, panicked and overwhelmed. But all of the sudden, amidst the moment of total panic, the Lord came into our living room. He was like a breath of air that stilled everything inside of me. He said four simple words: "Jocelyn, she is light." After a pause, he repeated the words, gently but firmly: "She is light."

I began to hear myself echoing all the things I said to Amber on our daily walks to school. Telling her who she was. Telling her to sow her heart. Telling her why she is there, in that school, with those people: because she is light.

How dare I freak out! Darkness looks for light, and my beautiful little light brought them, trapped in darkness, to my kitchen table. I can't shelter her from that. I have to walk with her in what it means to be light. I walk with her in her identity. I see it. I walk with her. I become it with her.

This is how we train our children. Our children are not just for mommy, daddy, or their family; they are for the world. I can't withhold her. Yes, it can be scary. There is no easy three-step plan to follow for a safe, manageable, guaranteed result. Our children are powerful people whom the Father has injected into our communities. They are for us, and they are for our world. We have to believe this.

So that night, when I went upstairs to tuck in our precious girls, I affirmed Amberle all over again in her identity. "Amberle, you are such a brilliant light. The way you love people is amazing. People crave the kind of love you have. They are hungry for it, and you have it. They are going to come to you and be loved by Jesus in you."

Though my mama bear instincts might be sorely tempted to set up protective boundaries that are based upon fear, I cannot walk in fear. I walk in love, fully persuaded of Jesus in my children. I walk with them in the true training that empowers and releases them.

In all the examples we have seen in Scripture about children, we can see how an adult saw and believed in the word of the Lord present in a child. Their agreement came into partnership with the child, opening or making way for the child's identity.

Think of Eli's posture toward Samuel. Remember Andrew's partnership with the boy with the lunch. When we read the story of Jehoash closely, we see that it was his aunt who saved him from death when he was only a year old, preserving him for the throne of Judah. She knew it was his identity to be king. (See 2 Kings 11) We need them, and they need us; without partnership, momentum cannot be gained.

The Seed and the Womb

We can see that from the very beginning there was a father and a mother, an Adam and an Eve, a seed and the womb to carry the seed. This is the nature of God in mankind. In the same way, within us lives both the image of God, as father and mother, the seed and the womb to carry it.

When a father gives a seed, there must be a womb or the seed dies. When I started thinking about that, I felt such an urgency in my spirit, and I began to rise up as a mother carrying children all over the world, not just my own. I began to pray and declare from my lips that not one will perish. My womb is open. The Bride's womb has to be open to receive the seed from the Father in all of our children. The spirit of the mother in you, which is in all of us, even men, opens our spiritual womb to carry.

Mary carried the seed of Jesus. We carry the seed of the Father. The Father gives the seed. The Father gives the identity, and He forms the child. There are so many Scriptures that talk about God forming us in the womb. *He formed me in my mother's womb. He knit me together. He called me a prophet to the nations while I was still in my mother's womb.* Even Paul said in Galatians that he was called from his mother's womb.

Intentionally, in our spirits, may we open our wombs. I don't care how old or young you are. Open your spiritual womb to carry, so that the Father can have the perfect environment to form. Isn't it beautiful? We carry both the spirit of the mother and the spirit and image of the Father in all of us. We carry the children of the earth so the Father can form them.

PRAYER

Father, thank you for our children. All of them. I thank you for the childlike spirit in us. May we never push it aside. May we lead as a child. I pray for fathers and mothers who are spiritual parents, as well as those who are natural parents of young ones right now, that they be encouraged and their eyes opened even more, every day, to who You are in their children. We open ourselves up to carrying many. May all of Your children be carried, believed in, and received. All. I say, not one will perish. Open the womb of Your Bride in the earth, to carry every one of them. For in them, we find You. As it says in Malachi, turn our hearts towards our children. We love you and we thank you for being such a good Daddy to us.

Specific Encouragement for Nursing Mothers

Psalm 22 is one of my absolute favorite psalms. I especially like this part:

Yet You are He who brought me forth from the womb; You made me trust when upon my mother's breasts. Upon You I was cast from birth; You have been my God from my mother's womb (Psalm 22:9-10).

When David wrote Psalm 22, he was in a time of distress. In the years when he was hiding or under attack, he could have looked back at any number of moments in his earlier life to say, "This is when I learned to trust the Lord." This is the guy who killed predators with his bare hands when he was a shepherd in the field. This is the guy who, as a young man, took out Goliath with a single shot. If I was David, trying to console myself in a time of distress, those are the big victories I would be reminding myself of. But David didn't say that. His consolation when he was in a rough place was, "Lord, I learned to trust You when I was nursing from my mama."

Mothers, if you are nursing infants, your children are learning to trust the Lord while you're nursing them. Do you see how beautiful this is? David learned to trust the Lord not in the great, crazy acts. Those things just *added* to what he already knew from the time he was drinking milk from his mother. I submit to you that we too learn to trust the Lord when we drink of Him. It's put to the test in the hard times, and we will see Him come through, but we learn His goodness when He holds us, and we drink of Him.

Train Them Up

It must be more than 1,000 times that I have heard people say that kids don't come with an instruction manual. But I tell you, every instruction is found in the heart of the Father. When you go into the Scriptures looking for His heart for children, you will find a wealth of it, way more than in any instruction manual. You find that it is in Him and in your child, in who they are.

Train up a child in the way he should go, Even when he is old he will not depart from it (Proverbs 22:6).

We train up the whole man. Not just behavior, but the whole person, body, soul, and spirit, in their identity, in full knowledge and belief in who Jesus created them to be. Training is at all times both spiritual and natural. In training our children, we must get the Father's heart for them. We hear the Father's heart, immersing ourselves in His thoughts for all children. Then we seek out our child's individual identity, for within their identity are the keys to training them up.

When we seek to learn the heart of the Father, He is faithful to reveal specific knowledge and understanding to us about our child. As we saw earlier, He has an identity placed on our children from the womb.

The Lord called Me from the womb; From the body of My mother He named Me. He has made My mouth like a sharp sword, In the shadow of His hand He has concealed Me; And He has also made Me a select arrow, He has hidden Me in His quiver. He said to Me, "You are My Servant, Israel, In Whom I will show My glory" (Isaiah 49:1b-3).

Later in the chapter, we read,

And now says the Lord, who formed Me from the womb to be His Servant, To bring Jacob back to Him... (Isaiah 49:5)

From the womb, there is a full identity within each child. Go to the Father and ask Him to show you what He was thinking about for your child when He formed that child in the womb. He says, "Ask and you will receive." Just ask. May He open your eyes to see and grow in your sight continually as you are with your children.

Abraham and Isaac

Abraham knew Isaac's identity. Before he was even conceived, God told Abraham, "You are going to have a son, and through this son, this promise is going to happen. This is who he is. This is his identity." This assurance is the only reason I can think of why Abraham had the resolve to obey God's instructions to sacrifice Isaac. He didn't freak out in front of Isaac. His roots were firm beneath him. He knew who his child was and was going to guide him in that way.

It is possible—and should be the norm—for us to get to know each of our children's identities very early on. Of course, we will grow in our understanding of who they are as they grow, but we can know their identities, just like Abraham knew Isaac's.

I knew part of Cara's identity when she was still in my womb. What the Lord said about her changed me before she was ever born. She released me to see in the spirit, and to experience dreams and angels. She released me into that before she was even born.

From a very young age, a child's spirit will respond to you. Sometimes we think that they have to become able to understand, but I tell you that before kids can even speak, their spirit knows the identity that's inside them. When you speak to their identity and their spirit, they will respond.

I want to tell you a simple little story. On Wednesday evenings, for a period of time, young Connor (only 16 months old) was in our class. He was newly learning how to walk, and was toddling all over the place. I would take his hand and walk across the parking lot with him while the kids played on the playground. We walked back and forth and back and forth.

One night, I started singing the song, *You Make Me Brave.* When I got to the part that says "You're a champion who made a way for all to enter in," I felt I was supposed to sing that over Connor. So as we walked, I started singing those words over him.

When he heard that line, he stopped abruptly and stared up at me. He didn't move. He wasn't going to leave that moment. I kept singing it over him because he wouldn't leave it. His spirit knew those words matched who he was. He was so young, too young to really even speak to me yet, but his spirit responded. Children respond. Their spirits are open and ready for us to join with them in who they are.

Isaiah and His Children

I love the way Isaiah saw his children. He was convinced that his children would be the marvelous acts and wonders that would call the people of the Lord to attention. When each of his children were born, Isaiah, seeing their power as infants, named each one a marvelous act before the child could even say mama or papa.

> *Behold, I and the children whom the LORD has given me are for signs and wonders in Israel from the LORD of hosts, who dwells on Mount Zion* (Isaiah 8:18).

Isaiah saw all his children this way. I see my children this way, and I see your children this way. Even more, Isaiah says he saw himself and his children as the marvelous wonders that would call to attention the remnant. We, together with our children, are this kind of wonder in the earth. Not us without them. Not them without us. It is us joined together with them that calls to attention the people of God.

Nurturing a Neighborhood Wonder

One day after school, all the kids in my neighborhood were out and about. I'm getting to know many of them. It is pretty common for me to have ten kids in and out of my house each day after school. Most of them are boys. Recently, we have had several conversations about anger. They struggle with how to handle it, so we have an open and ongoing dialogue. An opportunity soon came to us all, in shining colors.

Several of the boys came to my house in a huff, telling me there had just been a verbal explosion among the neighbor kids and one of their grandmas, who babysits one of them. Their words came out fast and confused, and I listened carefully, trying to put together a clear picture of the situation.

"My brother started cussing the girls out," one of them said, "and Grandma came out of the house yelling, and told us we were never allowed back on her property, Miss Jocelyn!"

They were extremely upset. I listened to the boys that had come to me and asked where all the others were, and where the grandma was now. Then I told them that we all love each other here. God gave us to each other as neighbors, to learn to love and work through things together. I offered my words in calm order, and the boys seemed to catch a deep breath.

Then we all got up, and they followed me out the door. Our mission was to go and talk openly and respectfully through things with the grandparent who had been so upset. As I walked down the alley, I saw several of the other boys, as well as the grandma, who was still piping hot with anger. Red-faced with rage, she yelled at us as we walked towards her. "Which one of those kids said the 'f' word to my granddaughter?! I want to know which one of you did it!"

As we approached her, I greeted her calmly and we all listened to her as she let out her anger. When her fury subsided, I opened up a conversation that all of us could be a part of, allowing her to observe and share in this dialogue with the boys. I shared with them that we all get angry sometimes, and we have all said things that we wish we hadn't said. I told them that we don't fly off and run from each other, but, instead, love each other enough to work through things.

One of the little boys spoke up. "My dad told me that if someone does something wrong to me, I should give it right back to them."

"Well, we are going to try a little something different today," I replied. "We are going to love each other. We are going to humble ourselves and apologize to each other and see what happens, because this is how we love. This is how we work things out."

We talked through what had happened, in order to understand why the blow up had erupted between the children, and whose hearts were hurt on both sides of it. In no time at all, they all began to apologize to each other and forgive one another.

The grandmother's jaw dropped, and she stared at me. I couldn't tell if she was angry with me or not. I just prayed that she could connect to where my heart was taking them, to the living example of love that was being set before these dear children, so that this experience of love would be forever etched in their minds and hearts. I knew these kids needed to see a living example of love that was courageous enough to open up, in a spirit of honor and respect, and work through the tough stuff.

With the angry storm settled among us all, we went our separate ways. As I was walking back to my house, two of these little boys opened up even more. The one who had become so hurt and angry that he threw the cussing words at the others, said, "It feels like that lady hates me."

It was the most honest thing he could have said. He opened up, and I could see his heart hurting. I talked with him about how he is such a good kid, a good friend, and a good big brother. We talked about what love and honor were, and that he could love and honor that lady, and that over time she would begin to trust his heart. You could tell this was hard for him. He gave me a hug and went off to play.

About an hour later, he came back to me with the huge grin on his face. Light danced in his eyes. "Miss Jocelyn, guess what! I talked with her! I was scared at first, and I almost just went away. But I made myself go over to her when I saw her outside, and I asked her if we could talk. I told her I didn't mean those things I said, and that I was sorry. She talked with me and told me it was okay, but that I can't say those things again. Now I can't stop smiling, Miss Jocelyn! I feel so happy inside!"

Tears welling up in my eyes, I ran to hug him and just hold him. I told him how proud I was of him, and how that it was Jesus in him that allowed him to respect her, honor her, and talk with her when he was scared that she hated him. I reminded him that he was a good boy. I sat down again, and he got on his bike, ready to head home. He looked at me for a few seconds, then said, "Miss Jocelyn, you tell me that I am good a lot." He stared off into the distance for an awkward pause, then murmured, "and every time you tell me that, I smile. No one else tells me that, that I'm a good kid."

His heart, his beautiful heart! What he said is true for a whole lot of children. There are so many kids who are never told that they are good. I weep for them. How precious they are, even when they don't know it! How precious and open and tender every one of them is, if we can just get to their hearts.

Believe it or not, in the evening of that same day, the grandmother who had been so upset called me. She apologized to me, then said, "You were teaching those kids how to not fight like adults do. You taught them how to do it right, how to love." I was awed and so very thankful to see and experience how much her heart had softened. My heart was so thankful, and my eyes were filled with tears all night. God's nearness and care for these dear people was tangible. He trusts us with their hearts and gives us the most incredible opportunities to walk with them. He is completely faithful to every single one.

The Father's Heart Turned Over Within Him

The Father's heart for all His children, old and young, is easily heard in Hosea. In chapter 11, we read,

When Israel was a youth I loved him, And out of Egypt I called My son. The more they called them, The more they went from them; They kept sacrificing to the Baals And burning incense to idols. Yet it is I who taught Ephraim to walk, I took them in My arms; But they did not know that I healed them. I led them with cords of a man, with bonds of love, And I became to them as one who lifts the yoke from their jaws; And I bent down and fed them. They will not return to the land of Egypt; But Assyria—he will be their king Because they refused to return to Me (Hosea 11:1-5).

Doesn't the Father's cry here hurt your heart? Whatever it takes, He, in His wisdom, realizes that He must allow them to get to a place where they will be as a child: choosing to come. It's gut-wrenching to read His cry further on in the chapter,

How can I give you up, O Ephraim? How can I surrender you, O Israel?...My heart is turned over within Me, All My compassions are kindled... (Hosea 11:8)

His whole heart is turned over within Him because He longed for His people, His children, to come to Him. It goes on,

I will not execute My fierce anger; I will not destroy Ephraim again. For I am God and not man, the Holy One in your midst, And I will not come in wrath. They will walk after the Lord, He will roar like a lion; Indeed He will roar And His sons will come trembling... (Hosea 11:9-10)

Can you hear the depth of His roar that would move them to come? So many times, we hear the roar of the Lord among us and we think that it is against us. But it is for us! Yes, even the discipline of the Father is not against us; it is for us. The Father among us, in His roar, in His passion and zeal, is not against us. He is for us. Oh, that we hear the roar of the Father among us which causes us to come to Him. May all of His children come.

The Father shows great patience toward His people. The first characteristic we read in 1 Corinthians 13 is that *love is patient.* Look here at the patience of the Lord. But His love is also passionate and jealous of our hearts to be fully His. His love is powerful. His roar is powerful. And when you hear that roar, it calls to attention everything inside of you. A holy fear of the Lord is experienced that actually draws us unto Him. Remember, children come. He beckons us, in our childlike hearts, to come.

Pushing Through the Process: Your Children are Worth It

Eve really messed up by eating the forbidden fruit. If there was anyone, who in their process of becoming could say, "I'm done. All I did was bring death; they are better off without me," it would be her. She probably felt completely disqualified. And yet, what did Adam name her? Even after she messed up (and of course we know that he ate that fruit too), he called her "the mother of all living." All living. Here we have this woman who was feeling the weight of doing the wrong thing, and all the consequences that went with her decision, and still Adam calls to her identity by speaking over her in that dark hour, "You are Eve, the mother of all living." She could not abort her process of becoming, even in the low place. She could not quit. In the same way, may we not stop short. May we too push through and allow the Lord to bring us up into who we really are.

I once experienced a vision where I saw the hands and feet of the Lord on the cross. They were bleeding. Just before this, I had watched as His hands tilled the soil of my heart. All of this resonated in my spirit. He encouraged me to surrender to His hands, bleeding with love, working, pressing, and shaping what was inside me. I have to. My children are interceding for me, so that I can give them life. That is what moms do. We give life.

Give, and it will be given to you (Luke 6:38a).

Give. Surrender. Give all you are and all you have to the Lord. Surrender to these hands that bleed with love. The verse continues,

they will pour into your lap a good measure—pressed down, shaken together, and running over (Luke 6:38b).

I give Him me. I surrender every part of my heart and my becoming to Him and to His process in my life for me, to call me up. And He will be faithful to press and to shake what needs to be shaped and shaken. He is going to homogenize me with Him in the shaking. We will be shaken together until we become one, and until all that needs to fall away from me falls away.

I want to give my all. Our kids are worth it. We want to give our all. Our descendants, the generations that will come from us, are worth it. He is worth it.

We can't stop short. No matter the process, whatever the pressing, whatever the shaking is, it is in your surrender to the hand of the Lord in the process that He is accomplishing. It is for them. As we are for them, they are for us. Hear them intercede for you. They really are carrying you.

PRAYER

Father, I thank You, for You with us, faithful to every part of us. I thank You for the promise. You in us. You in our descendants. You, our Promise. I pray for each heart. I pray for each spirit, for each mind. Every single one, at any point, when they feel like putting it down. When they feel like they have no more to give and want to just give up and quit. May we hear and may we see our descendants. May we hear the intercession of our descendants that is for us, that we would keep on, that we would press in. That we would be fully given, fully surrendered to You, Father, in the pressing and in the shaking, and that You would be allowed to complete the work in us that is for them.

PART FOUR

THE PROMISE

9

THE FUTURE

There are a lot of children in the earth today. Out of seven and a half billion people, it is estimated that two billion are children. Since over one fourth of our global population is children, it is critical that we accurately see the Father's heart for them, and, to take that one step further, see ourselves in them.

"Arise, walk about the land through its length and breadth; for I will give it to you" (Genesis 13:17).

It is time that we intentionally invest part of our days walking about the land that the Lord has promised to us. We have to take time with the Lord to see the land of our descendants. What will it to look like? The Lord longs to show us the land He is giving to us and our descendants. He urges us in the same counsel He gave Abraham: "Walk about the land, Abraham! Walk about this land through its length and breath. Walk through the entire thing. See it, for I will give it to you."

I do this a lot, and my heart deeply desires a company of people who will invest in our future generations in this way, rather than settling for one or two prominent leaders telling us what they see this land looks like. No, we are all going there, and seeing it with the Lord. We are not confined to seeing only today. The Lord sees all the generations. In Him, we too can see.

He obviously considered this important for Abraham. He told Abraham to do this. We must take time to do this as well. In our spirits, united with His, let's walk about the land, for He said He will give it to us and our descendants.

PRAYER

Father, I ask that the things that you show us would be so real to us that they would be more real to us than our skin. We want to see our children and our great-great-grandchildren through the blood of Jesus and through every promise of Your heart to us and our children.

We must take time to walk about the land.

The Lord is within children. He is speaking to them and will be released through them. He is already being released through them. I am convinced that this generation of children will literally change the face of the earth. The face of the earth will actually look different. That's how big this is. What our descendants inherit—and what they do with it—will change the face of the earth.

"Arise, walk about the land through its length and breadth; for I will give it to you" (Genesis 13:17).

I cannot stop walking about the land of our descendants. I see them all the time. Each time I go there, I am released to see just a little bit more. What I saw last week, last month, last year, seems small and incomplete as the details open wider to my heart. My sight keeps growing. The things I saw yesteryear seem so little compared to what I see now. I long to experience the more that I see. I am beginning to taste a freedom such as I have never known—but which will be the norm for our descendants. And I so want to live there with them.

One night, in the middle of the night, I woke up from a dream. I had built a small kids' rollercoaster in my backyard, and it was a hit! I was so happy listening to the laughter of kids and their wonder of it in my backyard! But that was nothing to what I experienced next in my spirit.

As soon as I sat up in bed, I saw children, in the purest spirit, in such knowledge of love, so completely connected to who the Lord is in them and the wonders that live within them. These children were practicing parting the waters in swimming pools! There was laughter and freedom. The wonders that Moses did were their playground of preparation for what would be in their future. Their freedom, their limitless living, literally moving mountains with such care and love and authority, literally releasing rain from the Heavens in every capacity.

Then I looked and it was night, and all I saw were flames of fire all over the earth. The places where you would expect darkness to be, like over the seas, were teeming with moving light. The movement of the children in the spirit was colorful light with pockets of fire within, and it was everywhere.

Movement. I can't even begin to explain the movement that I could both see and feel. The atmosphere was saturated with light and love and freedom. No place was untouched. There were no longer pockets of light. No, instead, the whole Earth was filled with hues of light, active and moving! It was 100 times greater than the pictures I had seen of the Northern lights—and the light was coming from *people*. I heard the ocean waves break on the rocks. I felt the core of the earth respond to our children every time their spirits made even the slightest movement in "I AM."

Our descendants will know a freedom that releases the natural world we live in to look like and be the physical representation of what we know already is in the Spirit. Everything that we have tasted in our spirits will be released to be embodied by the earth.

I am undone. My core craves the experience of what I see. This longing…I long to be one who will free the generations to live limitless and full in "I AM." I cannot even fathom the freedom that they will know, but just tasting it has my hunger so overtaken with desire for its substance in my belly.

Jesus, more! We want to see…really see. We agree with You, Papa. We receive the land of our descendants. We believe it. We believe they are real. We believe they are among us. Father, free us. We who think we are free…Oh Father, free even us, Papa. May the generations that come from us live *free!*

PRAYER

Father, we love our children—all of them.

We join our hearts to them. We receive them and believe all that You have said about them. We bless them with Your Person, forever full in them. We bless them with every bounty of Heaven. We bless them with wisdom and revelation and with favor. We honor Your nature in them and Your purpose within them for us and for the earth.

May they be tender and strong, relentless and free as they seek You and as they reveal You. May they be continually filled with the knowledge of You, of Your presence, and of Your nature so deeply that they cannot be shaken. May they cling to all that is good and right and pure. May they forever know and prefer Your voice, their hearts fastened to Your love and their eyes to Your face. May their faith be established and made sight even now!

Be their hope and their confidence, their full assurance from birth. Be their vision, everything in You so full and truly free, the impossible made possible.

We let them lead us and teach us and uncover in us our own childlike hearts. We will invest in them all that we are, for we believe who You have called them. We declare that they are sealed to Your love. We seal them to every promise and every purpose of Your heart for them and in them, Lord, for they are living wonders of Your great love and power in our world!

Oh, may they live full and fearless, limitless and free! May the earth see You and experience You because of these miraculous wonders among us today!

May the spirit of a child in the earth be set free to be filled with awe and wonder again, to know Jesus simply again. To love and believe, forgive and trust again. To explore and to imagine and to fearlessly lead the earth to its Father and Creator again! We call the earth to hear and to receive these, our children. For in them, in us, in the childlike spirit and heart, in the children of God young and old, is the sound of Heaven that the earth has longed for.

Written by Jovie, one of the children at our church,
during a worship gathering.

ABOUT THE AUTHOR

Jocelyn longs for the earth to see children the way the Father has showed her He sees them. She longs for people to be free to become as children, and she is fully convinced a childlike spirit will change the world. For more than 11 years Jocelyn has given herself to this vision and love of the Father for children. She practices what He has shown her with the children in her home, her community, her church where she is a children's pastor, and in several other nations. She shares this heart and vision through preaching, teaching, and workshops with churches, schools, parents, and ministries. Jocelyn and her husband, Chris, have three daughters and live in Pennsylvania.

RESOURCE RECOMMENDATIONS

www.achildwillleadthem.com

Visit our website for more stories of Jesus in children, helpful blogs, resources, and to connect with us.

Here I Am, The One You Love by Stephanie Schureman

If you're a parent of a young child, this book provides an easy, helpful platform to begin these simple conversations with your kids. This is a children's book that talks about children seeing visions and dreams, and how they can feel God's presence with them and hear His voice. If you struggle with how to talk with your children, this may help you get started. There are times where my children and I will read part of it and then spend time listening to each other's heartbeat.

Don't get too complicated in your adult mind; resist the temptation to overthink these things or to overanalyze everything. Remember: *Jesus is simple.*

eGenCo

Generation Culture Transformation
Specializing in publishing for generation culture change

Visit us Online at:
www.egen.co

Write to: eGenco
824 Tallow Hill Road
Chambersburg, PA 17202, USA
Email: info@egen.co

facebook.com/egenbooks
youtube.com/egenpub
egen.co/blog
pinterest.com/eGenDMP
twitter.com/egen_co
instagram.com/egen.co